This is the Word of the Lord

Year C

This is the Word of the Lord

Year C
The Year of Luke

EDITED BY ROBIN DUCKWORTH, SM

London
BIBLE READING FELLOWSHIP

Oxford New York Toronto Melbourne
OXFORD UNIVERSITY PRESS · 1982

Oxford University Press, Walton Street, Oxford OX2 6DP

London Glasgow New York Toronto
Delhi Bombay Calcutta Madras Karachi
Kuala Lumpur Singapore Hong Kong Tokyo
Nairobi Dar es Salaam Cape Town
Melbourne Auckland
and associate companies in
Beirut Berlin Ibadan Mexico City

Bible Reading Fellowship, St Michael's House,
2 Elizabeth Street, London SW1W 9RQ

British Library Cataloguing in Publication Data
This is the word of the Lord.
  Year C: The year of Luke
  1. Lord's Supper   2. Lectionaries
  I. Duckworth, Robin
  264'.3   BV825.5
  ISBN 0–19–826666–9

Library of Congress Cataloging in Publication Data
Main entry under title:
This is the word of the Lord.
  Contents: v. 1. Year A, the year of
Matthew.–   –v. 3. Year C, the year of Luke.
  1. Bible–Homiletical use.   2. Bible–
Liturgical lessons, English. I. Duckworth, Robin.
BS534.5.T46   264'.34   80–49921
AACR1
ISBN 0–19–826666–9

Typeset by Phoenix Photosetting, Chatham
Printed in Hong Kong

Contents

Names for Sundays in Ordinary Time

Some churchpeople will be familiar with other names for these Sundays not within the two great seasons. Whatever the titles used – Sundays after Epiphany, then Sundays after Pentecost, for example – the readings in the three-year scheme are substantially the same. In all the churches there is careful adjustment so that after the interruption by Lent–Easter the readings begin again together.

The table on page 43 supplies information which makes clear the set of readings to be used, no matter what title is common for Sundays out of season.

Readings in the Episcopal Church (USA)

The new Prayer Book's Lectionary fits with Sundays in Ordinary Time as follows:

Ordinary Time	Sundays after Epiphany	Propers
2nd	2nd	
3rd	3rd	
4th	4th	
5th	5th	
6th	6th	1 (closest to May 11)
7th	7th	2 (closest to May 18)
8th	8th	3 (closest to May 25)
9th		4 (closest to June 1)
10th		5 (closest to June 8)
11th		6 (closest to June 15)
12th		7 (closest to June 22)
13th		8 (closest to June 29)
14th		9 (closest to July 6)
15th		10 (closest to July 13)
16th		11 (closest to July 20)
17th		12 (closest to July 27)

18th	13 (closest to Aug. 3)
19th	14 (closest to Aug. 10)
20th	15 (closest to Aug. 17)
21st	16 (closest to Aug. 24)
22nd	17 (closest to Aug. 31)
23rd	18 (closest to Sept. 7)
24th	19 (closest to Sept. 14)
25th	20 (closest to Sept. 21)
26th	21 (closest to Sept. 28)
27th	22 (closest to Oct. 5)
28th	23 (closest to Oct. 12)
29th	24 (closest to Oct. 19)
30th	25 (closest to Oct. 26)
31st	26 (closest to Nov. 2)
32nd	27 (closest to Nov. 9)
33rd	28 (closest to Nov. 16)
Christ the King (Last Sunday of the Year)	29 (closest to Nov. 23)

Contributors

Mabel Bennett, Secretary of the Catholic Biblical Association of Great Britain. Eastertide

Kevin Donovan, SJ, Lecturer, Heythrop College, University of London. Liturgical introductions

Robin Duckworth, SM, Lecturer in Old Testament, Allen Hall, London. Year of Luke's Gospel; Acts; Psalms; Lent, Holy Week; 18th–23rd Sundays in Ordinary Time; Chronological Tables

David Gunn, Lecturer in Biblical Studies, University of Sheffield. 13th–17th and 24th–34th Sundays in Ordinary Time

Raymond Hammer, Director, the Bible Reading Fellowship. The Epistles; Apocalypse

Arthur McCrystal, Head of Theology, Newman College, Birmingham. Advent–Christmas

Arthur Moore, Vice-principal, Wycliffe Hall, Oxford. 2nd–12th Sundays in Ordinary Time

Acknowledgement

The Responsorial Psalms are reproduced from the Grail version, © The Grail (England) 1963, published by Collins in Fontana Books, London, 1963. Used by permission.

Forewords

As President of the World Catholic Federation for the Biblical Apostolate, I welcome this small, handsome, and very useful book. No doubt it will find its way into the hands of priests and catechists as a valuable tool for the preparations of Sunday homilies.

But I sincerely hope also that it will reach many of the faithful. It is to them in particular that I wish to recommend this book highly. Reading the short commentaries on the Sunday readings and Gospels will greatly assist a deeper understanding of the texts, and in this way the Liturgy of the Word will become a more effective tool for evangelization.

⛌ Paul Cardinal Zoungrana
President of W.C.F.B.A.

The adoption of the Three-Year Cycle of Readings in many churches around the world has opened the way to a more widely-based reading and exposition of the Scriptures at the Eucharist. We are finding it has great ecumenical significance too: it is splendid that Christians of different traditions are reflecting upon the same passages of the Bible on the same day.

The Bible Reading Fellowship is doing a valuable service to the clergy and laity alike in providing the helpful pithy commentaries on the weekly readings which are set out in this book.

I am very happy to commend this practical aid to our deeper appreciation of the eucharistic readings.

⛌ Keith Rayner
Archbishop of Adelaide

Preface

This book is primarily for layfolk who wish to come to a better understanding of the content and message of the passages of Scripture used in the Sunday Lectionary. The method employed has been to explain simply and clearly what the passages are about and to place them in their context. To do this the commentators have tried, as far as possible, to let the readings 'speak for themselves', so that the reader may obtain maximum benefit from them. Because personal interpretation has been avoided it is hoped that the explanation of the texts will be of special value to individuals and study groups who are seeking to understand the text without being 'led' to a particular interpretation.

The supplementary sections have been added in order to give the user of the book a broader general base from which to work. There is an introductory article on this year's Gospel, Luke, and also on the Acts of the Apostles. The same author wrote both accounts and they are obviously closely related. Passages from Acts are used for some of the readings during Eastertide. There is a survey of the epistles which occur in the readings and also of the Apocalypse. As the Responsorial Psalms are printed out within the commentary – both as a convenience and as an aid to devotion – the introduction has a brief survey of the background and content of the Psalms. It is hoped that the chronological tables will enable words and events to be set in their historical context. The maps provide a 'geographical context' which may be found helpful when meeting place names and for locating the 'churches' to whom Paul wrote his letters. The brief book-list will encourage those who wish to pursue subjects further.

Finally it should be remembered that Scripture is the word of God passed on to us in the words of men who lived at a particular time and in their own cultural environment. To know something of the background and context of the readings contained in the Lectionary paves the way for a better understanding of these 'words of men', which in turn, it is hoped, will lead to a greater awareness of the 'word of God'.

Robin Duckworth

INTRODUCTION

Year C: The Year of Luke's Gospel

The Lectionary devotes to each year of its three-year cycle one of the synoptic Gospels ('synoptic' means 'from the same viewpoint', and the first three Gospels are called synoptic because, broadly speaking, they look at their subject from the same point of view). Supplementary material is taken from the Gospel of John. Each Gospel does, however, have its own particular approach to the teaching of Christ, and it is by concentrating on a single Gospel throughout the liturgical year that the particular approach of each evangelist can be best appreciated. Year C is devoted to the Gospel of Luke.

Tradition is unhesitating in ascribing both the third Gospel and the Acts of the Apostles to St Luke. Present-day scholarship also, in general, is satisfied that the author of these two books could have been Luke, the disciple and companion of Paul. Luke dedicates his Gospel to a certain Theophilus, a man of some social standing as the title (Excellency) given to him shows. Tradition had it that such patrons were expected to promote the works dedicated to them. It is also evident from a study of the Gospel that Luke wrote for the Gentiles. He consistently avoids many matters which may appear too Jewish. He also omits or changes details that do not redound to the credit of the apostles. These things have been explained from the fact that because Luke was addressing Gentiles, and especially Greeks who were prone to discussion and criticism, he did not want to raise difficulties for them.

Characteristics

In his gospel account Luke keeps to the same general plan of the other two synoptics, namely: the ministry of John the Baptist and the inauguration of Jesus' ministry; the Galilean ministry; the journey to Jerusalem; the events in Jerusalem. In fact Luke makes Jerusalem the pivot of his whole Gospel. Jerusalem is the Holy City of God and it is there that the great redemptive event, the passion and triumph of Christ, will take place. The Gospel begins in Jerusalem (1: 5) and there it ends (24: 52f.). The climax of Salvation History takes place there, for there Jesus died and rose again and from there he ascended into heaven. Consistent with this theme we find in Luke's second book (Acts) that it was from this same centre, Jerusalem, that the Christian message spread out 'to the ends of the earth' (Acts 1: 8) (see below).

Luke makes two important changes in the original four-fold gospel plan mentioned above. He balances the Passion Narrative with an Infancy Narrative at the beginning, and he introduces a long section, peculiar to this Gospel, into the Journey Narrative. We have seen Luke's pre-occupation with Jerusalem, and the material that he adds to the journey section shows that Luke is dealing with more than a merely geographical itinerary; it is rather a spiritual pilgrimage leading up to the passion and triumph of Jesus Christ. Thus the Gospel may be divided into the following general sections:

5. Jerusalem Ministry   19: 29–21: 38
   Messianic entry, teaching in the Temple, summary of last days of Jesus.

6. Passion and Resurrection   22: 1–24: 53
   From events culminating in Jesus' arrest to Ascension, and return of the apostles to Jerusalem.

Theology

As we have seen, Luke was writing for Gentile Christians and so he
stressed the universal aspect of the gospel. The angels announce the
Saviour's birth bringing 'peace to men of good will'. Simeon predicts
that the child Jesus will be a 'light of revelation to the Gentiles'. Luke
(unlike Matthew) takes the genealogy of Jesus back to Adam, the
father of mankind. The command of Jesus to the Twelve not to go
among the Gentiles or the Samaritans on their mission (Matthew 10:
5f.) is omitted by Luke. The Jews are warned that at the Messianic
Feast they will be supplanted by men from every nation. The last
command of Jesus (24: 47) is that the gospel should be preached to all
nations.

Related to this universal aspect is Luke's stress on Jesus as the
Saviour of mankind. The title is used only once: 'to you is born this
day . . . a Saviour' (2: 11), but Luke draws special attention to the
name given to the child at his circumcision: Jesus (which means
Saviour) (2: 21). Throughout Luke's record Jesus is seen as a
Saviour full of tenderness and compassion and forgiveness. Thus
Luke's Gospel can be called a Gospel of mercy. This is very well
illustrated by the three mercy parables of chapter 15: the lost sheep,
the lost coin and the prodigal son. The last two are found only in
Luke's Gospel. In the forgiving of the 'woman who was a sinner',
Jesus' words to the self-righteous Pharisee are unequivocal: 'Her
sins, which are many, are forgiven, for she loved much' (7: 47). It is
Luke alone who records the words of Jesus to the good thief (23: 43)
and his prayer for his executioners (23: 34). This theme of forgiveness permeates the whole Gospel.

The sensibility of Luke is brought out by his attention to women,

3

especially since, in his day, women were very much second-class beings. Not only are a number of women mentioned in the Gospel, but two parables (found only in Luke) concern women: the lost coin (15: 8–9) and the unjust judge (18: 1–8). Of all the women mentioned, however, it is Mary the mother of Jesus who is highlighted, particularly in the Infancy Narrative.

This Gospel of mercy also shows concern for the poor and the humble, beginning with the angels' message to the shepherds and ending with the pardoning of the good thief. This preoccupation with the materially and spiritually poor is repeatedly made evident: 'the Son of Man came to seek and save the lost' (19: 10).

Luke's Gospel is also a Gospel of prayer, the great model and example of which is Jesus himself. He prayed before his baptism, when he retired into the wilderness, before choosing his apostles, before Peter's profession of faith. He prayed at the Transfiguration, and he prayed on the Cross. Our Lord also recommended prayer to his disciples, especially persevering prayer, which he illustrated by the parables of the friend who came at midnight (11: 5–13), and the widow before the unjust judge (18: 1–8). Not only must their prayer be sincere, like that of the publican (18: 13), but they ought to pray at all times (21: 36). And what is more, they must pray to obtain the Holy Spirit (11: 13).

The Holy Spirit also receives special notice in Luke's Gospel. Jesus as Messiah is the bearer of the Holy Spirit. It was 'in the power of the Holy Spirit' that Jesus began his messianic work. Other important characters in the Gospel are either moved by or filled with the Holy Spirit: Mary, John the Baptist from his mother's womb, Zechariah, Elizabeth and Anna. Luke's Gospel is about mission, obedient sharing in the activity of the Holy Spirit. Among his last instructions to his disciples Jesus tells them to stay in Jerusalem where 'you shall receive power when the Holy Spirit has come upon you' (Acts 1: 8). It is to the beginning of Acts that we must turn to hear how that power came upon them.

The Acts of the Apostles

The intimate connection between the Gospel and Acts is brought out by the two recordings of the Ascension (Luke 24: 50 and Acts 1: 9). We have seen how in the Gospel everything leads to Jerusalem where the redemptive triumph of Jesus will take place. In the Acts of the Apostles we see a corresponding movement away from Jerusalem with the spreading out of the news of that redemption. The key to the whole book is to be found in 1: 8 '. . . you shall be my witnesses in Jerusalem and in all Judaea and Samaria and to the end of the earth' (that is, Rome). It is particularly in this last part that the guidance of the Holy Spirit becomes evident. What Luke is concerned to impress upon his readers is that the mission to the Gentiles is the expressed will of God. And at every stage of expansion there is to be found the intervention of the Holy Spirit: when Peter receives the first Gentile into the Church (ch. 10) and Paul accepts his mission to the Gentiles (ch. 9); it is by the Spirit that Paul is sent on his first missionary journey (13: 2–4); it is the Spirit who leads Paul to Greece (16: 6–9) and finally on the journey that ends in captivity in Rome (20: 23). With Paul's arrival in Rome the goal has been reached and the command of the departing Jesus fulfilled.

Though the theme of Acts is the geographical expansion of the Church, its growth in numbers and self-understanding, the book is, nevertheless, rich in theological content. The doctrine of salvation is set out quite simply. The basic elements are: Christ alone brings salvation. This salvation is effected by Christ's death, resurrection and exaltation. It is described as forgiveness of sins accompanied by repentance. It is obtained through faith accompanied by baptism. It must be preached first to the Jews, but will be accepted principally by the Gentiles. All the basic doctrine we profess concerning Christ can be found in Acts, along with teaching on the sacraments of Baptism and the Eucharist. We have seen the important place of the Holy Spirit in the life of the Church. We see above all the growth of that Church in response to the command of Jesus and the inspiration of the Spirit. It is thus significant and appropriate that the Acts of the Apostles is a source-book for many of the liturgical readings in Eastertide.

Year C: The Epistles

Whilst the Old Testament reading and the Gospel set the theme for the Sunday readings, the Epistles are important for us as emphasizing the lines of continuity between ourselves and the early Church. The Epistles were simply letters written to the early Christian communities or their leaders and provide us with a glimpse of what the life and worship of the early Church was like and the kind of problems they were facing or the questions they posed.

The Sundays in Ordinary Time provide us with readings from many of the shorter letters in the New Testament, but 1 Corinthians (which was also drawn upon for Year A and Year B) is used as well – as it clearly illustrates the care and concern shown by Paul for a church that he had himself established. Where only selections of the letters are chosen for the second reading at the Mass, it is recommended that groups and individuals read up the passages omitted to get a more complete picture. In Ordinary Time the selections are as follows:

Sundays 2–8	1 Corinthians 12–15
Sundays 9–14	Galatians
Sundays 15–18	Colossians
Sundays 19–22	Hebrews 11–12
Sunday 23	Philemon
Sundays 24–26	1 Timothy
Sundays 27–30	2 Timothy
Sundays 31–33	2 Thessalonians

We shall also take a look at the Apocalypse and Titus, as they are drawn upon for the second reading in the Festal Seasons. In the main, however, it is only in Ordinary Time that the lectionary provides the opportunity for a more regular reading of this important area of New Testament writings.

1 Corinthians 12-15

Paul first visited Corinth after his brief visit to Athens (see Acts 18: 1ff.). His first preaching there was in the Jewish synagogue, but, later, his work was almost exclusively among Gentiles. Most of the new converts belonged to the lower classes and some of their attitudes reflected the low moral standards and intense rivalries which were features of life in Greece's chief port. Chapter 12 stresses that it is one and the same Spirit who is responsible for the wide variety of gifts that people have. All Christians have their part to play in the body. Paul ridicules the situation where we try to do someone else's work. We need to recognize our own function in the life of the whole. Chapter 15 is Paul's lengthiest teaching on the Resurrection. He gives the evidence for Christ's resurrection and argues that that is the basis of confidence in our own future resurrection.

Galatians

It is likely that Galatia refers not to Galatia proper, where the people were Celts, but to Lycaonia to the south (still part of the Roman Province of Galatia), which had been visited and evangelized by Paul in his first great missionary journey (see Acts 13 and 14). The chief cities involved were Pisidian Antioch, Iconium, Derbe and Lystra. It seems that some Christians with Jewish background were aghast that so many Gentiles had received baptism and became church members without identifying with Judaism and its initiatory rite of circumcision first. Paul has been the object of abuse and attack and he draws upon his own conversion experience to explain the reason for his approach to the matter. In 4: 20 he says that he does not know which way to turn; on the one side, he stands for freedom from the demands of the Jewish Law, but, on the other, he is not advocating moral laxity. On the one side, he is fighting for the freedom of the Gentiles to enter the Christian fellowship without becoming Jews first, but, at the same time, he is deeply concerned for the unity of the Church, where Christians of Jewish and Gentile background are members together of the family of Abraham whose faith had commended him to God. There were those who thought that dependence on 'faith' meant that it did not matter what they did. Paul asserts that baptism leads to the indwelling of the Spirit and that his presence in the Christian is responsible for the production of the different virtues, the 'harvest of the Spirit'.

Colossians

We do not know whether Paul actually visited Colossae. But it was not far from Ephesus and it is likely that the church there came into being as the result of evangelistic outreach from Ephesus. As in the other letters, doctrine and moral teaching are intermingled, our conduct being the inevitable consequence of what we believe.

First of all, Paul is concerned to establish the Colossians in the true faith, in the face of false teaching. Next, he instructs them in the Christian way of life. In the third place, he is anxious to foster the sense of community in the church, asking for mutual love and harmony, whilst, lastly, there is the personal touch – news of fellow-Christians in Rome and the sending of greetings.

Hebrews 11–12

These chapters in a letter by an unknown writer are concerned largely with faith and perseverance. Faith is seen as that which undergirds hope and assures us that we are not living in a world of fantasy. This has been true of all the Old Testament heroes who now surround us, as we 'run our race' – and on the track ahead of us is Jesus, who not only provides us with a basis for faith, but is also the goal towards which we advance. Christians, as *they* face persecution, are assured that they belong to a kingdom which cannot be shaken.

Philemon

This is the only personal letter of Paul which survives. Philemon was a leader in the Colossian church, and his slave, Onesimus, had run away. He had met Paul and become a Christian and Paul is now sending him back. The name 'Onesimus' means 'useful' or 'profitable', and Paul indicates that one who had been 'useless' is now truly 'useful'. He points out, too, that 'slave' and 'master' are really equal before Christ, because he is the true 'master' of both.

The Pastoral Epistles (1 and 2 Timothy, Titus)

This title has been given to these letters because both Timothy and Titus feature as young men called to positions of leadership in the

Church and requiring direction from the old apostle Paul how best they are to exercise their pastoral oversight. Whilst they were accepted as written by Paul from the time of Irenaeus (about AD 200) onwards, most modern scholars regard them as later compositions which incorporate genuine fragments of Paul's own letters. We can imagine a writer at the end of the first century AD asking 'What would Paul be saying to us, if he were alive today?' Far more important than the question of authorship are the content and teaching. All three letters are concerned with the kind of leader who is a dedicated minister of Jesus Christ, preserving the faith, teaching incisively and engaging fervently in evangelism. Both Timothy and Titus are pictures of the ideal Bishop! The letters urge us not to be so concerned with structural trivialities that we neglect the fundamental task in which the Church's ministry is engaged. And yet the letters do teach that a structure is important if the Church is to survive the onslaught of false teaching. Tradition is important, too, for the word means 'handing-on'. Each age is called to *'hand on'* the faith to the next age – but this means (say the Pastorals) that we must first know it for ourselves.

2 Thessalonians

Thessaly was the name given to the territory south of Macedonia and north of Greece proper. Paul had established a church at Thessalonica during his first visit to Europe, as he journeyed south from Philippi to Athens. Two of his letters to the church there survive and, by comparison with 1 Thessalonians, the second letter is very sombre and formal. There is far more emphasis on judgement than on hope for the faithful! A threefold aim seems to mark the letter. Paul is concerned: 1. to encourage and strengthen his readers to stand steadfast in their faith despite persecution; 2. to elucidate the meaning of the 'Day of the Lord' – the Old Testament name for the time of God's judgement; and 3. to suggest patterns of discipline in the life of the church.

The Apocalypse (Revelation)

'Apocalypse' comes from a Greek word which conveys the idea of *removing a covering*. The notion is that there is much which is *covered up* for us or *hidden* from our understanding, but that God himself *uncovers* (or *reveals*) the truth for us. So the author of the book ('John') is a prisoner on the island of Patmos because of his Christian faith and might well have felt that the tiny Christian churches he knew in Asia Minor (now part of Turkey) by the coast of the Aegean Sea could not fight with the might of the Roman Emperor. The *revelation* he receives convinces him that the truth of the situation is that it is God and not the Roman Emperor who is in control of history and that God's will for the renewal of the world and of humanity will prevail. Jesus (pictured as 'the lamb') had died, but, now risen, he is alive for evermore and, what is more, is in control of the destinies of all. With God he receives the worship and adoration of heaven and earth.

The message is one of 'no compromise' and 'perseverance' members of the Church are urged to be faithful to their commitment. Only through perseverance can they reach the final goal of history.

The writer draws upon the figurative language of the Old Testament books Ezekiel and Daniel, as he speaks of the downfall of Rome (the new Babylon, which once again attacks Jerusalem, not the earthly city, but the eternal city of God). The earthly conflict is seen as having its counterpart in the heavenly sphere, where evil is finally defeated. The New Jerusalem is a picture of heaven, where there is no more parting or sorrow, where everything is renewed and the light comes from Christ, the only Sun.

Of course, the language is meant to be poetical and not literal, for the book introduces us to a reality which cannot be described in ordinary language. Special note should be taken of the large number of early Christian hymns included in the book.

The Psalms

From very ancient times, language in the form of poetry with musical accompaniment has been used in the liturgy of communal worship. And so there have evolved intoned poems of prayer with each one taking a traditional form according to its place in the sequence of worship. The Psalms of the Bible are poems or songs (the Greek word *psalmos* means a song) of this kind surviving from Israelite worship.

Little is known about the history of the collection of Psalms as we have it today. It is generally estimated to have been completed in the fourth century BC. The collection is in five divisions, though there are signs within these of earlier groupings. Smaller sequences of Psalms have been gathered together for various reasons. They may have been connected in liturgical usage, or belonged to the repertoire of a certain guild of Temple musicians, or they may simply have resembled one another in theme or worship. Gradually all these groups were gathered together into the present structure of the book of Psalms.

Though it is not possible to date accurately the individual Psalms, it can be deduced, both from the connection with Jerusalem and the monarchy, and from comparison with other Old Testament and extra-biblical material, that the main period of composition was in the time of the Davidic Dynasty (i.e. about 1000–587 BC). The roots of the tradition, however, go back into earlier Israelite and Canaanite worship, while its growth continues into later times.

The Psalms would normally have been composed and sung by the Temple personnel. These belonged to guilds and orders of sacred ministers, some of whom would have specialized in psalmody and music. Sometimes the kings themselves composed Psalms (David, in fact, is noted in tradition as the author of many), though it would have been more normal for the king to have had the royal prayers composed for him by a member of the Temple orders or guilds. At the very least, David was responsible for a collection of Psalms being made.

There was an appropriate type or class of composition for each situation in worship where a Psalm might be used. Themes, express-ions and structure followed the convention of the types in question. Many of the present Psalms are grouped into such classes. Others, however, though having many of the traditional features, are less easily classified. Much recent and modern scholarship has been devoted to studying this classification with the result that a great deal has been added to our understanding of the Psalms and their place in Israel's worship. A pioneer in this field of study was the German scholar Hermann Gunkel. By means of a classification of types, largely following the thought, mood and vocabulary in the different Psalms, Gunkel has tried to fit these Psalms into what may have been their original setting. What follows is a summary of the main categories of his classification.

Psalm types

Laments make up the largest single category of Psalms. They may be individual in character (e.g. Psalms 3, 5, 7, 13) or communal (sometimes called 'national') (e.g. Psalms 44, 74, 79). Individual laments seem to be the prayers of individual sufferers, in which there is a cry for help, a description of the sufferings or dangers encountered, and often an indication that there are enemies whom the sufferer wishes to see overthrown. There is usually an expression of confidence that God has heard the prayer and will act upon it. Regular stock images are used to describe both the plight of the sufferer and the character of the enemies at whose hand he is suffering. Communal or national laments usually incorporate cries to God to hear and come to the people's rescue. There is normally a description of the plight of the people which is intended to stir God to compassion, and a call for his judgement on their oppressors. Often there is an appeal to God's promises in the covenant he has made with Israel, and, once again, an expression of confidence that God has heard the prayer.

Thanksgiving Psalms also may be individual (e.g. Psalms 30, 32) or communal (e.g. 67, 124). Individual ones will express the kind of trouble from which the psalmist has been delivered, whilst the communal ones will refer to some particular national deliverance.

Hymns form a large class (e.g. Psalms 33, 145–150). They emphasize the element of praise, or of reverence and joy in God's presence. The reason for the call to praise and exaltation is usually given. Within this group occur the *Songs of Zion* (e.g. Psalms 46, 48) which are concerned with the Holy City, and the *Enthronement Psalms* (e.g. Psalms 47, 96–99) in which God is proclaimed King.

Royal Psalms (e.g. Psalms 2, 18, 110, 132) point to special events in the reigns of kings before the destruction of the Temple in 587 BC. There may be references to the king's enthronement, his wedding, his anniversary or some such important occurrence.

Pilgrimage Psalms (sometimes called 'gradual' Psalms) (e.g. Psalm 84, 121–134) were used by companies of pilgrims as they went up to the Temple in Jerusalem for the annual festivals.

Wisdom Psalms (e.g. Psalms 1, 73) form one of the smaller groupings and, like the Proverbs, often point to the contrasting destinies of the just and the wicked. *Torah liturgies* (as in Psalms 15 and 24) convey priestly instruction or provide liturgical dialogue, whilst *Prophetic liturgies* (as in Psalms 60 and 75) point to an oracle given by a prophet.

Alphabetical Psalms are Psalms in which each stanza begins with a consecutive letter of the Hebrew alphabet. The most impressive example is Psalm 119; in every stanza the first letter of each verse is the same, and there are twenty-two stanzas, one for each letter of the Hebrew alphabet. Psalms 111 and 145 are simpler examples.

The numbering of the Psalms

The numbering in this book's commentary and articles follows that which is used in most modern Bible translations. Liturgical books have tended to follow the numbering of the Septuagint (the Greek translation of the Old Testament). There, because some Psalms were merged (9 and 10) and another divided (147), a scheme arose which differed from that of the Hebrew Bible. For most of the psalter (11–146) the Hebrew counting is one ahead of the Greek; also, Psalms 114–116 are differently divided.

Hebrew	Septuagint and Vulgate
1–8	1–8
9–10	9
11–113	10–112
114–115	113
116	114–115
117–146	116–145
147	146–147
148–150	148–150

The Responsorial Psalms are printed out in full in this book, not only for ease of reference, but to provide groups and individuals with material for their prayerful response to the readings. (The Greek or liturgical number of the Psalm is given in brackets after the usual biblical one.)

Seasons I

Seasons I

ADVENT

Liturgical Introduction

'As we wait in joyful hope for the coming of our Saviour, Jesus Christ . . .' – these words are the special theme of Advent, a season of waiting. The Church's year ended on the note of Christ's Kingship and Second Coming. This is continued into the new Advent. This theme was particularly dear to the earliest generations of Christians. 'Maranatha, come Lord Jesus,' they sang at every Eucharist. Has our expectation grown dim as the centuries between his first coming at Bethlehem and his final coming seem to lengthen? Sombre world events and domestic tragedy remind us of our need for a Saviour and the hope he generates. Unlike the Old Testament figures of the readings, we know that our Saviour has already come. But we still have to welcome him into our lives. Stay awake, prepare the way of the Lord. There is the Baptist's insistence on repentance, and Paul's assurance that God will keep us steady – he began the good work in us and will bring it to completion. The Lord is near, and will bring us his peace. And so we pray that God will increase our power for doing good, and will remove the things that hinder us – especially the sadness that prevents our experiencing the joy and hope which Christmas should bring.

As the feast draws closer, we focus more on the people and events surrounding our Lord's birth and infancy. Mary is especially prominent. It is her faith that Elizabeth praises, and our prayers now ask that we may imitate her self-dedication. We meet strong references to Christ's self-offering and loving obedience. The crib leads to the cross, and then beyond to the resurrection and final glory. This is God's plan for the whole world. We are drawn into Christ's sacrifice and, even in Advent, ask that we may share in his suffering and death so as to enter into his glory.

At Christmas itself, the emphasis is more directly on Christ's birth, God's coming to us in visible form, to enlighten our darkened world and lead us to share in his divine life. The weekday readings from St John's letter stress that this must involve loving one another. We have to recognize and welcome Christ into our lives in many ways. Family life, on the model of Jesus, Mary and Joseph, is naturally stressed. The Christmas season ends with Christ's baptism – another revelation of Jesus, this time as servant. This path too we are called to follow. Advent does not usher in an idle wait.

First Sunday of Advent

Despite present trials – discouragement, distress, slander and anxiety – those who remain faithful have every reason to feel confident that they will be vindicated. Justice and integrity will be established with the coming of the Son of Man.

First Reading   **Jeremiah 33: 14–16**

The author recalls God's promise to the people of Israel and Judah that a virtuous king would arise amongst them and that he would be a man of honesty and integrity. When that time arrives peace will come to Judah and security to Jerusalem. Such a promise implies a criticism of the historical situation but carries with it also encouragement to have confidence that God, through the activity of the expected king, will bring about both virtuous behaviour and deliverance from their present predicament. The same promise also occurs in Jeremiah 23: 5–6. The passage in today's reading is different from this in two ways (verse 16): Jerusalem instead of Israel and the name 'The Lord our Integrity' is given to Jerusalem rather than to the person of the king. There is general scholarly agreement that our passage is a later addition to Jeremiah, dating probably from the time of Zechariah (c. 520 BC) or of Malachi (c. 500 BC); both were periods of discouragement and dissension. This later addition quoted Jeremiah 23: 5–6, which appears to have its historical context in the reign of Zedekiah. This king's name etymologically signifies 'integrity' and 'salvation' or 'deliverance'. It would be the role of the future king to bring about the promise inherent in Zedekiah's name.

Responsorial Psalm   25 (24)

℟ *To you, O Lord, I lift up my soul.*

1 Lord, make me know your ways.
   Lord, teach me your paths.
   Make me walk in your truth, and teach me:
   for you are God my saviour. (R)

2 The Lord is good and upright.
   He shows the path to those who stray,
   he guides the humble in the right path;
   he teaches his way to the poor. (R)

3 His ways are faithfulness and love
   for those who keep his covenant and will.
   The Lord's friendship is for those who revere him;
   to them he reveals his covenant. (R)

A prayer in time of distress. The author is encouraged as he thinks
of God's goodness and fidelity.

Second Reading   **1 Thessalonians 3: 12–4: 2**

Paul probably wrote this first letter to the Thessalonians about the
year 51. Timothy had brought him very encouraging news (perhaps
a letter) about the church which he had, a short time previously,
founded there. Paul gives thanks for the love which the Christians in
Thessalonica show to one another and he prays that the Lord may
increase their mutual love and that they will extend that love to the
'whole human race'. This latter request was very difficult for them
since their fellow-countrymen are hostile to them (1: 15). In Paul's
thought, however, persecution can be expected if one is a Christian
(3: 3, 4 , 7). The Thessalonians are to grow in holiness as they await
the coming of Christ; Paul reminds them of the standards of behaviour to which the Christian is called.

Gospel   **Luke 21: 25–28, 34–36**

Luke here paints a picture of the fear and distress of men when they
are faced with cosmic disaster – when they live under threat of the
destruction of the universe. Mark's Gospel has a parallel treatment

of the same theme (Mark 13: 24–26). Both Luke and Mark identify the Son of Man with the risen Jesus. With his coming men will be delivered from their fears and anxieties. During the period of waiting for their risen Lord, however, Christians should be careful to avoid being coarsened by indulging the darker desires of human nature. In contrast to the pagans, Christians can face the day of judgement with confidence as they stand before the Son of Man who has overcome all the cosmic forces of evil.

Second Sunday of Advent

There is high expectancy that the Day of the Lord is coming soon: it is the day of salvation for all men – mourning, distorted judgement, and sin will be removed.

First Reading   **Baruch 5: 1–9**

This section of Baruch cannot be dated earlier than the first century BC. Jerusalem is portrayed as a beautiful woman who is told to put off her garb of mourning and dress to suit this joyful occasion, when she sees her children returning from their captivity. God gives her a new name which will be hers forever: 'Peace through integrity and honour through devotedness'. Last Sunday the name given to her was 'Lord-our-integrity'; today we have a similar picture. The peace that comes to Jerusalem is the result of her upright life and her glory is the result of the *fear* of God (the Vulgate translates fear as *pietas*, devotion). The author of Baruch uses the imagery found in Isaiah 40: 4–5 to describe the homecoming of the people to Jerusalem their mother. 'Every valley shall be lifted up and every mountain and hill made low. . . .'

Responsorial Psalm   126 (125)

℞ *What marvels the Lord worked for us!*
Indeed we were glad.

1 When the Lord delivered Zion from bondage,
It seemed like a dream.

Then was our mouth filled with laughter,
on our lips there were songs. (R)

2 The heathens themselves said: 'What marvels
the Lord worked for them!'
What marvels the Lord worked for us!
Indeed we were glad. (R)

3 Deliver us, O Lord, from our bondage
as streams in dry land.
Those who are sowing in tears
will sing when they reap. (R)

4 They go out, they go out, full of tears,
carrying seed for the sowing:
they come back, they come back, full of song,
carrying their sheaves. (R)

A song in the form of a lament (cf. p. 12). The time of the joyful
return to Jerusalem is contrasted with a later period, that of the
Psalm, when enthusiasm has waned; but the author looks to another
joyful time to come.

Second Reading   **Philippians 1: 3–6, 8–11**

Paul is writing shortly before his death. In his prayer he remembers
the enthusiasm with which the Philippians helped him to spread the
gospel. The Philippians had remained faithful since Paul first went
there. God will continue his work amongst them until the day when
Christ will return. Originally Paul had hoped to be alive when that
day came (1 Thessalonians 4: 15; 1 Corinthians 15: 51) but now he
sees that he will not live so long. He prays that their mutual love may
increase; he feels that his love for the Philippians is Christ's love
present to them. But the people of Philippi do have short-comings; it
is only an increase of love that will purify their judgement as to real
values. Then when the Lord comes he will find nothing to condemn in
them. But more than this, they must allow Christ to produce now a
fruitful Christian life in each of them.

Gospel   **Luke 3: 1–6**

This year's Gospel describes the beginning of the ministry of John the Baptist. Both Luke and Mark in the parallel passage (Mark 1: 2–5) regard the mission of John as the 'beginning of the gospel of Jesus Christ'. Luke synchronizes his account of John's ministry with the political and ecclesiastical history of the time. 'The fifteenth year of Tiberius Caesar's reign' corresponds to AD 28–29. Mark (1: 4–5) situates John's ministry as well as his call in 'the wilderness'; Luke depicts him as a wandering prophet in 'the whole Jordan district' (cf. also Luke 7: 24). Mark and Luke use Isaiah 40: 3, as did Baruch, but they introduce certain small adjustments in the text which present John as the Herald of Christ, and Luke expands the quotation by a few words from Isaiah 40: 5, namely: 'all flesh shall see the salvation of God'. Luke wishes to emphasize the significance of Christ for the salvation of all men.

Third Sunday of Advent

The Lord is very near – so near that the joys of the Messianic age can be anticipated in our celebration.

First Reading   **Zephaniah 3: 14–18**

Zephaniah is traditionally regarded as a seventh century BC prophet and a citizen of Jerusalem (1: 4). The verses of today's reading, however, are generally recognized as late: they paint a picture of the final golden age, which is thought to be near at hand. Israel's time of trial has passed. The author lays great emphasis on the presence of God with his people: he is 'in their midst' as a warrior who brings victory and also, in his love, renews his people. Jerusalem's saviour will feel towards his city as a bridegroom for his bride, as he comes to his city amid dancing and shouts of joy. The passage is imbued with the spirit of Second Isaiah (Isaiah 40–55) – there is security in the presence of the Lord.

Responsorial Psalm   **Isaiah 12: 2–6**

℟ *Sing and shout for joy*
for great in your midst is the Holy One of Israel.

1 Truly, God is my salvation,
   I trust, I shall not fear.
   For the Lord is my strength, my song,
   he became my saviour.
   With joy you will draw water
   from the wells of salvation. (R)

2 Give thanks to the Lord, give praise to his name!
   make his mighty deeds known to the peoples!
   Declare the greatness of his name. (R)

3 Sing a psalm to the Lord
   for he has done glorious deeds,
   make them known to all the earth!
   People of Zion, sing and shout for joy
   for great in your midst is the Holy One of Israel. (R)

Brief psalms from Isaiah 12, beginning with thanksgiving for deliverance and moving on to more general praise. We have cause for
joy.

Second Reading   **Philippians 4: 4–7**

The Philippians await the coming of the Lord. Paul encourages them
in that hope – 'the Lord is very near' – although he now believes that
he will not live until that day. Christians, as they wait for this
coming, should be characterized by joy as they undergo their trials.
They are to be fair-minded (tolerant) and flexible – not insisting on
their rights. Their conduct and beliefs were strange to their pagan
neighbours, consequently they must be patient as they find themselves misunderstood. Continual prayer will be their safeguard
against anxiety as they live in hope of the coming of the Lord. God
will give them his peace – the knowledge that he is with them. This
will guard their hearts and their thoughts.

Gospel   **Luke 3: 10–18**

This passage falls into two sections. In the first, which occurs only in

23

Luke, the Baptist gives ethical advice to various groups of his followers. The rich should share with the poor; the tax collectors should not practise extortion; soldiers – probably those who provided an armed guard for the tax collectors – should not intimidate civilians. The second section is paralleled in the other three Gospels and it portrays John's understanding of the mission of the Messiah. It is his task to separate the evil from the good as a farmer separates the wheat from the chaff. The Baptist contrasts his baptism (by water) with that of the coming Messiah, which will be 'with the Holy Spirit and fire'. Luke gives especial prominence in his Gospel to the role of the Holy Spirit. Often in the Old Testament God's spirit is portrayed as having a special role to play in Messianic times (e.g., Joel 2: 28 (3: 1) 'After this I will pour out my spirit on all mankind'). John describes the baptism which the Messiah gives as also being 'with fire'. The Spirit cleanses and purifies as the wind blows away the chaff. Luke regards John's announcement of the coming of the Messiah as a preaching of the gospel.

Fourth Sunday of Advent

A new messianic king will come; his life will be characterized by obedience to the will of God; God has been true to his promises. Mary has been rewarded for her faith; the Messiah is alive in her womb.

First Reading   Micah 5: 1–4

The prophet Micah flourished around the last years of the eighth century BC but the book which bears his name has aptly been described as, 'a source book for observing the development of Hebrew thought from 714 BC to approximately 200 BC'. Today's reading goes back to the origins of the Hebrew monarchy. Bethlehem was five miles southwest of Jerusalem and it was situated in the region known as Ephrathah. It was an insignificant village and yet out of it came David, whose destiny it was 'to rule over Israel'. Then the text moves to the time of the exile. The exile itself is seen as God's abandonment of Israel and it lasts until God will choose to bring forth a new king – the woman who will give birth is Israel. The kingship will be restored and the people will return; the new king will care for his people. Moreover this restored kingship will have no end – a new world empire will come about and all people will acknowledge the divinely instituted king.

Responsorial Psalm   80 (79)

℞ *God of hosts, bring us back;*
  let your face shine on us and we shall be saved.

1 O shepherd of Israel, hear us,
   shine forth from your cherubim throne.
   O Lord, rouse up your might,
   O Lord, come to our help. (R)

2 God of hosts, turn again, we implore,
   look down from heaven and see.
   Visit this vine and protect it,
   the vine your right hand has planted. (R)

3 May your hand be on the man you have chosen,
   the man you have given your strength.
   And we shall never forsake you again:
   give us life that we may call upon your name. (R)

A plea for help in time of distress. The people are likened to an unprotected vine, but they are confident that God will help. They pledge faithful conduct in the future.

Second Reading   **Hebrews 10: 5–10**

The author quotes Psalm 40 (39): 6–8 as an expression of Christ's attitude to God when he came into the world. His life is to be characterized by his obedience to the will of God. This obedience is presented as far superior to any animal sacrifice. The Greek (Septuagint) version of Psalm 40 (39): 6 reads: 'you have fashioned a body for me'. The author of Hebrews takes up this idea and applies it to Christ's body being sacrificed. But it is his obedience which is the essence of his sacrifice. The purpose of sacrifice is 'to make holy'. God's will for us is that we should be made holy by obedience to him: thus we lead a life of sacrifice.

Gospel   **Luke 1: 39-44**

An old tradition situates the summer house of Zachary and Elizabeth at the village of En Kerem about 2½ miles west of the outskirts of Jerusalem. This makes En Kerem (the sping of the vineyard) the 'town in the hill country of Judah' to which the Gospel refers. 'The Visitation' has many messianic features: the child in Elizabeth's womb leaps joyfully as the poor will dance (Isaiah 35: 6; Malachi 4: 2 (3: 20)); Elizabeth gives 'a loud cry' as in Isaiah 40: 9 – 'Shout with a loud voice, messenger to Jerusalem'. The unborn Baptist recognizes the unborn Messiah; Elizabeth also recognizes him and she emphasizes Mary's faith in God's promises.

CHRISTMAS DAY

Midnight Mass

Power to bring about true peace marks out the ideal king of Israel.
Jesus Christ has made such peace possible: he is the ideal king from
David's line who will bring peace to the whole world.

First Reading   Isaiah 9: 2–7

This poetic passage is an oracle which was most probably composed
by Isaiah for delivery during the anointing ceremony of a new king.
The prophet sketches the qualities of the ideal king who is to come
from the royal Davidic line. Many of the motifs found in this passage
occur also in Psalms related to the Davidic dynasty – dawn of a great
light, the overthrow of the king's enemies (cf. the allusion to Gide-
on's total victory over the Midianites, Judges 6–8), the establishment of the throne in a place which will last for ever. The titles given
to the new king depict him as sharing in the divine attributes of
wisdom, courage, constant care for his people, and the power to
bring about true peace. Christian tradition understands this ideal to
be fulfilled in Jesus Christ.

Responsorial Psalm   96 (95)

℟ *Today a saviour has been born to us;*
  he is Christ the Lord.

1 O sing a new song to the Lord,
  sing to the Lord all the earth.
  O sing to the Lord, bless his name. (R)

2 Proclaim his help day by day,
  tell among the nations his glory
  and his wonders among all the peoples. (R)

3 Let the heavens rejoice and earth be glad,
  let the sea and all within it thunder praise,
  let the land and all it bears rejoice,
  all the trees of the wood shout for joy
  at the presence of the Lord for he comes,
  he comes to rule the earth. (R)

4 With justice he will rule the world,
 he will judge the peoples with his truth. (R)

A Psalm from the enthronement of Yahweh (the Lord) as king (cf. p. 12). Two motifs stand out in this excerpt. Firstly, Israel is invited to praise God for his wonderful deeds in creation. Secondly, all creation is invited to celebrate God's reign over it.

Second Reading   Titus 2: 11–14

According to this letter Titus presided over the church on the island of Crete. The letter is clearly written to instruct Titus as to how he should organize the Christian community. The author indicates that there are many 'who need to be disciplined, who talk nonsense and try to make others believe it' (1: 10). Our excerpt emphasizes the role of Jesus Christ: he 'has made salvation possible'; he is 'our great God and saviour'. People in Crete lived amongst the sin of the world – they are 'liars, dangerous animals and lazy' (1: 12). Christ sacrificed himself 'to set us free' from this sinful predicament, to purify a people so that it would have 'no ambition except to do good'. The title used of Jesus – 'our great God and saviour' – seems to reflect Christian polemic against the emperor cult and the mystery religions. Our author claims for Jesus the divine titles which the pagans claimed for their gods. But more than this, functions which are ascribed to God in the Old Testament are ascribed by our author to Jesus (e.g., the purification of a nation to be his own).

Gospel   Luke 2: 1–14

St Luke attempts to set his account of the birth of Jesus into the context of secular history. The attempt, when examined against what we know from other sources about this period of history, seems to be chronologically inaccurate – but it does highlight Luke's intention of portraying the universal significance of Jesus: he is part of world history. Luke appears to have believed that Mary and Joseph were natives of Galilee, whereas Matthew presumes that Jesus was born in Bethlehem because Mary and Joseph lived there. Both Matthew and Luke stress the Davidic descent of Jesus and both imply that his birth took place at night. Luke, with his shepherds' story, has the birth proclaimed to people in a traditional but now despised occupation. The description of Jesus as *saviour* introduces a central theme in Luke's theology. The term does not occur in Mark and Matthew: in the Old Testament God is called *saviour* (Isaiah 43: 3; 45: 15; cf. Luke 1: 27). Our passage ends with a proclamation of Jesus as Messiah similar to that by the people when he triumphantly entered Jerusalem (Luke 19: 38). God's 'peace' can be identified with Luke's understanding of *salvation.*

Dawn Mass

God has released his people from their captivity; they are 'regenerated', born into the new life of the messianic age. It is by the life of the Messiah that this has become possible. He has been born today.

First Reading   Isaiah 62: 11–12

This short excerpt must be seen in its context in Third Isaiah (Isaiah 56–66): it is a song of return from the exile. The author is clearly a disciple of Second Isaiah because this song is woven from quotations from the latter. These verses catch the spirit of such celebrations as the Feast of Tabernacles. The author sees a multitude of pilgrims singing and dancing in Jerusalem and his thoughts turn to the Diaspora: he longs for their return to the holy city. He pictures God coming as a victor with 'his trophies before him': he comes as king of his people. They are the holy people of the holy God, he has redeemed (released) them from captivity. Jerusalem which has earlier been described as 'forsaken' (cf. 62: 4) is now 'The-sought-after'. God has made for himself a new people.

Responsorial Psalm   97 (96)

℟ *This day new light will shine upon the earth:*
the Lord is born for us.

1 The Lord is king, let earth rejoice,
  the many coastlands be glad.
  The skies proclaim his justice;
  all peoples see his glory. (R)

2 Light shines forth for the just
 and joy for the upright of heart.
 Rejoice, you just, in the Lord;
 give glory to his holy name. (R)

A Psalm of the Lord's enthronement (cf. p. 12): a song of praise to
God for his great justice. This justice is reflected in the upright of
heart.

Second Reading   Titus 3: 4–7

Titus 3: 4–7 gives the theological basis for the Christian's behaviour
being different from that of the non-Christian. In verse 3 the author
recalls the behaviour of the people of Crete prior to their becoming
Christians: he lists their vices: 'ignorant, disobedient and misled
and enslaved by different passions and luxuries: we lived then in
wickedness and ill-will, hating each other and hateful ourselves'. It
was precisely to save them from this sort of life that 'the kindness and
love of God our saviour' appeared. The initiative for man's salvation
came totally from God. That salvation is brought about through
baptism and it is an act of God's compassion. Through baptism we
are born into a new life – *regenerated*. This last word occurs elsewhere
in the New Testament only in Matthew 19: 28; there it refers to the
messianic age. Having been *regenerated* the Christian can live a new
style of life – 'sober, upright and godly' (2: 12).

Gospel   Luke 2: 15–20

Several phrases in St Luke show his conviction that God's revelation
is often made to very humble people: e.g., 1: 52 'He has pulled down
princes from their thrones and exalted the lowly'; 6: 20 'How happy
are you who are poor: yours is the kingdom of God'; 7: 22 '. . . the
Good News is proclaimed to the poor'.

 This last phrase is one of the signs of the messianic age which Jesus
points to in his reply to the question put to him by the disciples of
John the Baptist. It is no wonder then that Luke should choose the
motif of shepherds in his infancy narrative. We can remember too
that the Patriarchs were shepherds, as was David. In the two verses
(13–14) immediately preceding our gospel text the shepherds are

depicted as having witnessed the heavenly liturgy. They now go over to Bethlehem to verify what the angel has told them (2: 10). The angelic message and the heavenly liturgy enable the shepherds to understand that the child they find in Bethlehem is indeed the Messiah.

Day Mass

The herald brings good news: the Son of God having destroyed sin has taken his place at the right hand of his Father; he has overcome the powers of evil (darkness) and shares with those who accept him this same power to conquer darkness.

First Reading   Isaiah 52: 7–10

The author here describes the coming of God to Zion, his holy city. His thinking is shaped by his belief that *the Day of the Lord* would come, bringing with it the abolition of all misery and suffering. The scene depicts a herald striding over the mountain and watchmen on the walls of ruined Jerusalem waiting to hear the news that he brings. Our author knows that the news he brings is good – peace, happiness and salvation – and so he tells the ruined city to 'break into shouts of joy'. The time of Jerusalem's redemption has come; God 'bares his holy arm' as he prepares to restore and protect the city – his saving power will be clear for all the nations of the world to see. God's action in Jerusalem is his manifestation of his power to the world.

Responsorial Psalm   98 (97)

℟ *All the ends of the earth have seen*
the salvation of our God.

1 Sing a new song to the Lord
   for he has worked wonders.
   His right hand and his holy arm
   have brought salvation. (R)

2 The Lord has made known his salvation;
   has shown his justice to the nations.

He has remembered his truth and love
for the house of Israel. (R)

3 All the ends of the earth have seen
the salvation of our God.
Shout to the Lord all the earth,
ring out your joy. (R)

4 Sing psalms to the Lord with the harp,
with the sound of music.
With trumpets and the sound of the horn
acclaim the King, the Lord. (R)

A hymn of praise to God for the salvation which he achieved for
Israel and which now affects the whole world.

Second Reading   Hebrews 1: 1–6

The author of Hebrews describes his work as 'words of advice' (13:
22). He writes to prevent apostasy amongst those to whom he
addresses himself. Our text sets us firmly in 'the last days' and
Christians are described as those who have experienced 'the powers
of the world (age) to come' (6: 5). If, after this experience, they fall
away, 'it is impossible for them to be renewed a second time' (6:4)
because they have rejected Christ who as 'Son of God' is the central
reality of these 'last days'. This age in which we now live is characterized by the fulness of divine revelation made by *the Son*. He has
brought about our release from the power of evil, he has 'destroyed
sin' and consequently he has gone to take his place at 'the right hand
of divine majesty'. There he exercises an eternal high-priesthood;
he, and not any angel, is the true priest. The characteristic title of
Jesus is 'Son' and it carries with it a designation of Christ's pre-
existence as well as his having become 'Son of God' in the fullest
sense at the resurrection.

Gospel   John 1: 1–18

Our gospel reading for this Mass forms the prologue to John's
Gospel in its entirety. It is a poetic text which presents the various
themes which will be taken up in the rest of the Gospel. Jesus is the
creative word of God who was present with God at the beginning of

creation. Through him all things came to be. Now he is the final and full revelation of God. Within the godhead he is a distinct Person (cf. his claim to be *sent by the Father:* 7: 28–29; 8: 42; 16: 28) with an essential share in the divine life. Life, to be true life, has to be a sharing in the divine life. That life is considered as a light: it is the antithesis of darkness, which embraces all that is in opposition to God. John the Baptist came to be a witness to Christ who is the light. The world, which in John's terminology stands for all that is sinful and dark, was incapable of recognizing Jesus, but some people did accept him and to these he gave the power to become children of God. The word became flesh (i.e., he became fully human) and lived amongst us ('pitched his tent amongst us'). Just as God once dwelt with the Israelites in the Tent of Meeting (Exodus 25: 8; Numbers 35: 34), so now the divine Son lives amongst men as a real man of flesh and blood. Yet he remains 'the only Son of the Father'.

Holy Family (Sunday in Christmas Octave)

First Reading   Ecclesiasticus 3: 2–6, 12–14

Ecclesiasticus would appear to have derived its name from its close association with the Church (*the church book*). It was widely used in the early Church and its canonicity was frequently attested by the early church writers although it was not definitively made part of the canon of Scripture until the Council of Trent. It is also known as Sirach – the name of its author. A native of Jerusalem, Sirach was a highly respected person – a scribe and teacher, a man of means, a man who travelled much. In later years he ran a school in Jerusalem – the curriculum seems to have been a mixture of Scripture and worldly teaching. It is generally agreed that the book was written 195–168 BC. It is a blend of religious teaching and secular wisdom. Our reading emphasizes the traditional Jewish understanding of duty to one's parents; Sirach sees this duty as a consequence of our fidelity to God. The text is a commentary on Exodus 20: 12, 'Honour your father and your mother so that you may have a long life in the land that Yahweh your God has given to you'.

Responsorial Psalm   128 (127)

℟ *O blessed are those who fear the Lord*
   and walk in his ways!

1 O blessed are those who fear the Lord
   and walk in his ways!
   By the labour of your hands you shall eat.
   You will be happy and prosper. (R)

2 Your wife like a fruitful vine
   in the heart of your house;
   your children like shoots of the olive,
   around your table. (R)

3 Indeed thus shall be blessed
   the man who fears the Lord.
   May the Lord bless you from Zion
   all the days of your life! (R)

A song of Ascents (cf. p. 13); a wisdom Psalm in which the psalmist
points to the rewards which come to those who faithfully practise
their faith – peaceful enjoyment of the fruits of one's labour, many
children, and Jerusalem's remaining prosperous.

Second Reading   Colossians 3: 12–21

Part of the background to the opening verses may have been the
ceremony of baptism. Paul stresses the new life which the Colossians
should live now they are 'the people of God' (chosen . . . holy . . .
beloved). He summarizes the description of Christian love which we
find in 1 Corinthians 13: 4–7 and he does this by listing five social
virtues – compassion, kindness, humility, gentleness and patience.
Relying on their own experience of being forgiven by God, Christians must in their turn practise forgiveness. The image of putting on
love as a garment may derive from the baptism ceremony, where the
new life was symbolized by the putting on of the baptismal robe.
Peace is a gift from God. Family life would appear to be regarded as a
community life, which is to be characterized by the same quality of
life as the wider Christian community.

Gospel   Luke 2: 41–52

The final sentence of today's Gospel helps us to understand why Luke included this story of Jesus in the Temple. He presents Jesus as increasing 'in wisdom, in stature, and in favour with God and men' – the description here would appear to be based on that of the boy Samuel (1 Samuel 2: 26). He grew in all ways – he learned, he developed physically, he grew in graciousness, charm and tact. But there is also the element of mystery as the twelve-year old speaks of a special relationship to his Father: 'Did you not know that I must be busy with my Father's affairs?' Mary and Joseph are depicted as not understanding what he meant.

Mary, Mother of God (1st January)

The Old Testament formula of blessing invites God to be present to us; through the life-giving Spirit of Jesus we live freely in God's presence; the historical Jesus 'born of a woman' has brought about our freedom.

First Reading   Numbers 6: 22–27

The last sentence of this reading portrays God as saying that his name is to be called down upon the Israelites, according to a liturgical formula. According to Old Testament thinking, God's name is synonymous with God himself; hence we can infer that this priestly blessing is intended to invite God's presence amongst the people. The blessing is a prayer that the expectations of the people may be fulfilled – good crops and herds, suitable weather, victory in battle, protection from enemies. A shining face is a sign of the divine favour and graciousness: the uncovered (uplifted) face of God is a sign that the bonds of friendship have not been broken and so true peace can come about (2 Samuel 2: 22, Job 22: 26).

Responsorial Psalm   67 (66)

℞   *O God, be gracious and bless us.*

1 God, be gracious and bless us
   and let your face shed its light upon us.

So will your ways be known upon earth
and all nations learn your saving help. (R)

2 Let the nations be glad and exult
for you rule the world with justice.
With fairness you rule the peoples,
you guide the nations on earth. (R)

3 Let the peoples praise you, O God;
let all the peoples praise you.
May God still give us his blessing
Till the ends of the earth revere him. (R)

A song of thanksgiving for the harvest. God's goodness manifest in the harvest given to the Israelites is available also to the other peoples of the world.

Second Reading   Galatians 4: 4–7

This excerpt occurs in the context of a discussion on Christian freedom. Prior to the coming of Christ man was enslaved to the elemental spirits of the world (4: 3). But now that God has intervened in Jesus Christ we have been redeemed from the Law by that same Jesus who submitted himself to the Law. His life-giving Spirit enables us to be adopted as sons and so we are able to speak to the Father as Jesus did: 'Abba, Father'. We would be incapable of addressing God in that way if we did not have the Spirit of Christ. This brings the Christian true freedom.

Gospel   Luke 2: 16–21

The shepherds have experienced a theophany (2: 9–15): an angel of the Lord has come and announced to them news which will cause great rejoicing – 'today in the town of David a saviour has been born to you, he is Christ the Lord'. Luke's theological interest appears here in his designation of the infant as 'saviour'; he is also 'Messiah' and 'Lord' – this last is a title which the Old Testament reserved for God. With Christ a new era has come. When the theophany ceases the shepherds decide to go to Bethlehem and see the promised sign. They find everything as they have been told. The final sentence of today's Gospel refers to Jesus' circumcision, but Luke's primary interest is in the giving of the name – Jesus – 'the name the angel had given him before his conception'. Luke derived his description of Jesus as 'saviour' from the etymology of his Hebrew name.

Second Sunday after Christmas

Wisdom dwelt with God but has now come to abide in Israel; we need a spirit of wisdom if we are to appreciate God's eternal plan: 'No one has ever seen God; it is the only Son . . . who has made him known.'

First Reading   Ecclesiasticus 24: 1–2, 8–12

Chapter 24 is the central chapter of Ecclesiasticus. It is, as the Greek subtitle says, a 'eulogy of wisdom'. Wisdom is personified and portrayed as the first thing that God made. Then she played an intermediate role in the entire work of creation. It is in Israel that wisdom dwells in a special way; but before she came to Israel she had her throne 'in a pillar of cloud'. The pillar of cloud in the desert was the symbol of God's presence (cf. Exodus 13: 21–22): wisdom dwelt with God. She recalls her service in the Temple – 'the holy tabernacle' – and points out her presence in Jerusalem and amongst the entire people of Israel.

Responsorial Psalm   147 (146–147)

℟ *The Word was made flesh,*
  and lived among us.
  or *Alleluia!*

1 O praise the Lord, Jerusalem!
  Zion, praise your God!
  He has strengthened the bars of your gates,
  he has blessed the children within you. (R)

2 He established peace on your borders,
  he feeds you with finest wheat.
  He sends out his word to the earth
  and swiftly runs his command. (R)

3 He makes his word known to Jacob,
  to Israel his laws and decrees.

He has not dealt thus with other nations;
he has not taught them his decrees.
Alleluia! (R)

A hallelujah Psalm in which God is celebrated as the liberator of Israel – he strengthens her defences and establishes peace on her borders. Israel has special knowledge of God's Law.

Second Reading   Ephesians 1: 3–6, 15–18

The section of Ephesians from which this reading comes (1: 3–3: 21) has as its overall plan the expounding of a mystery. This mystery is God's plan to make Christ the head of a new brotherhood of man which will embrace both Jew and Gentile. It was part of God's plan from the beginning; Jesus Christ is its central figure: the brotherhood is constituted by being 'in Christ' – a phrase which occurs more than thirty times in the entire epistle. Being 'in Christ' we have access to salvation, we share in Christ's unique sonship. Once God's eternal plan is understood then it is so wonderful that it demands our praise. The author has heard of the Ephesians' great faith in the Lord Jesus and of their great love for their fellow-Christians (the saints). The author prays that the Christians of Ephesus may come to appreciate God's eternal plan which calls for the removal of social and racial barriers.

Gospel   John 1: 1–18

This prologue in the form of a hymn gives an account of how divine life is brought to the Christian. The account begins with the Word of God present with God from the beginning. There is a special relationship between the Father and the Word. All that the Father has created has intimately involved the activity of the Word – all things have been created through him. Since the Word is involved in the creative activity of the Father then that activity itself is an act of revelation. What has especially come to exist through God's creative Word is the gift of eternal life. This life is the light of men. John the Baptist is portrayed as a witness to the light. This light has come into the world to enlighten men as Isaiah hoped (Isaiah 9: 2): 'the people who walked in darkness have seen a great light . . .' The activity of the Word in the world has enabled men to become God's children.

'The Word was made flesh' and 'from his fulness we have all of us received.' God's covenant love has remained constant. It has been made manifest in the Mosaic Law, and now in Jesus Christ. He is the Word incarnate.

Epiphany (6th January, or Sunday between 2nd and 8th)

The glory of God shines upon Jerusalem; all nations are attracted to her glory. In God's eternal plan Jew and Gentile are to be members of the one body of Christ. The Gentile Magi came to pay homage to the infant king of the Davidic line.

First Reading   Isaiah 60: 1–6

Dawn is about to break over Jerusalem: 'night still covers the earth' but the sun is rising. This imagery symbolizes the new age which is about to dawn – instead of the sun it is 'the Lord' who is rising in Jerusalem, and the nations are shrouded in a metaphorical darkness. The author calls on Jerusalem to reflect onto the nations the *glory* of God which God shines upon her. Then once again Jerusalem is invited to look around – her children are coming home: she looks radiant. Great wealth, too, will come to her. Finally, the poet chooses imagery (camels, dromedaries) to suggest the vast wealth which will come to Jerusalem.

Responsorial Psalm   72 (71)

℟ *All nations shall fall prostrate before you, O Lord.*

1 O God, give your judgement to the king,
   to a king's son your justice,
   that he may judge your people in justice
   and your poor in right judgement. (R)

2 In his days justice shall flourish
   and peace till the moon fails.
   He shall rule from sea to sea,
   from the Great River to earth's bounds. (R)

3 The kings of Tarshish and the sea coasts
shall pay him tribute.
The kings of Sheba and Seba
shall bring him gifts.
Before him all kings shall fall prostrate,
all nations shall serve him. (R)

4 For he shall save the poor when they cry
and the needy who are helpless.
He will have pity on the weak
and save the lives of the poor. (R)

A prayer for a king, this Psalm is dedicated to Solomon. It celebrates his wealth, glory and peaceful reign. Solomon was respected and sought out by foreign rulers (cf. 1 Kings 10).

Second Reading   **Ephesians 3: 2–3a, 5–6**

The author presents the practice of allowing Gentiles to become Christians without first being circumcised, as a great eternal plan in the mind of God. It is a mystery which has been hidden from all eternity but which was made known to Paul by a 'revelation'. Pagans are now to share the same inheritance as the Jews. Both Jew and Gentile are members of the Body of Christ and they share the same realized promise of the Holy Spirit (1: 13). The bitter divisions of mankind are healed.

Gospel   **Matthew 2: 1–12**

This story of the visit of the Magi to Bethlehem has no parallel in any other Gospel or indeed in any other first-century Christian writing. It is easy to see why Matthew included it. The Magi fall to their knees and 'do homage' to Jesus. Matthew wants to show that Gentiles too have found their way to pay homage to the infant king of the Davidic line. The Magi were a well known and respected group of 'wise men' and it was popular belief that Hermes was their founder. They ask in Jerusalem about the star-sign which has brought them to Israel. The information they want is contained in the scriptural text from Micah 5: 2(1), which is interpreted by 'the chief priests and the scribes of the people'. Does Matthew regard them as the Magi of Israel? In later

Jewish literature Moses and Solomon are ranked amongst the Magi and Moses is depicted as taking the place of Hermes. The scribes' interest contrasts with that of Herod, who plays a similar role to that of the dragon in Revelation 12. There the murderous dragon waits, but the child is 'taken up to God while the woman escaped into the desert' (12: 6). Jesus was taken by Mary and Joseph to Egypt as a place of safety.

Baptism of the Lord (Sunday after 6th January)

The Servant works quietly at his commission to 'bring true justice'. Jesus is God's agent in removing evil from the world; he is the head of a new Spirit-filled community which continues his mission.

First Reading   Isaiah 42: 1–4, 6–7

Isaiah 40–55 contains four such songs as this. The Servant is Israel, present through history in the persons of her great leaders and in the suffering exiles (52: 13–53: 12). Later Judaism gave these songs a messianic interpretation. It is the kingly role of the Servant which is given emphasis here: he is 'the chosen one' who is commissioned to 'bring true justice'. He carries out his mission quietly and with gentleness – 'the crushed reed' is not broken. God's covenant with Israel is the basis of her mission to the world: she is made the light which shines in the spiritual darkness of the surrounding world.

Responsorial Psalm   29 (28)

℞ *The Lord will bless his people with peace.*

1 O give the Lord you sons of God,
    give the Lord glory and power;
    give the Lord the glory of his name.
    Adore the Lord in his holy court. (R)

2 The Lord's voice resounding on the waters,
    the Lord on the immensity of waters;
    the voice of the Lord, full of power,
    the voice of the Lord, full of splendour. (R)

3 The God of glory thunders.
  In his temple they all cry: 'Glory!'
  The Lord sat enthroned over the flood;
  the Lord sits as king for ever. (R)

A hymn to the Lord of the storm. The storm is a source of comfort and assurance. If God can work the wonders which we experience in a storm, then he can guarantee peace to his people.

Second Reading   Acts 10: 34–38

Peter has, a short time previously, experienced his vision of the great sheet 'let down to earth by its four corners' and containing various kinds of animal and bird – a choice of ritually unclean food (10: 10–16). Through this vision Peter has learned that 'God does not have favourites'. Peter's speech to Cornelius and those around him is adapted to a Gentile audience: '. . . anybody of any nationality who fears God and does what is right is acceptable to him'; Jesus Christ is 'Lord of all men'. The Baptism of Jesus is presented here as an 'anointing' of Jesus through the Holy Spirit. For Luke Jesus is God's agent who, filled with the Holy Spirit, devotes himself to 'doing good' and working for the destruction of evil as he cures those who have 'fallen into the power of the devil'.

Gospel   Luke 3: 15–16, 21–22

Two matters are dealt with here – the messianic preaching of John the Baptist and the story of the Baptism of Jesus. Jesus is 'mightier' than John – as 'mighty' he is the leader of the final struggle with evil (cf. Luke 11: 20–22). Luke merely mentions the fact of Jesus' Baptism and he never mentions John by name in his account of it. The early Church seems to have been embarrassed by Jesus' submission to the baptism of John. In Luke's account of the coming of the Spirit upon Jesus he is at prayer: the Holy Spirit descends upon him in bodily form, 'like a dove'. The dove represents the new people of Israel, of whom Jesus is constituted head by the coming of the Spirit. This episode may also point ahead to Pentecost, when the Holy Spirit will be poured out on the Christian community.

(Next Sunday's readings are on p. 93)

Note on Sundays in Ordinary Time

The first Sunday in Ordinary Time is always the feast of the Baptism of the Lord. The other Sundays then follow until Lent supervenes; the sequence begins again on the Sunday after Trinity Sunday. However, the sequence does not recommence exactly where it left off. (This gives the flexibility essential because years vary in their number of Sundays and in the position of Easter.) Either two or three Sundays are omitted in any one year. The table shows which these will be.

Sundays in Ordinary Time

Years	5	6	7	8	9	10	11	12
1983	6 Feb	13 Feb	—	—	—	5 Jun	12 Jun	19 Jun
1986	9 Feb	—	—	—	1 Jun	8 Jun	15 Jun	22 Jun
1989	5 Feb	—	—	28 May	4 Jun	11 Jun	18 Jun	25 Jun
1992	11 Feb	18 Feb	25 Feb	3 Mar	—	—	—	21 Jun
1995	5 Feb	12 Feb	19 Feb	26 Feb	—	—	18 Jun	25 Jun

Seasons II

LENT

Lent sounds negative, a time for giving things up. But new life is its goal, the new life of grace. Historically, it grew out of the final weeks of preparation spent by adult converts before their baptism at Easter. Christ's forty days in the desert, and Israel's forty years before crossing the Jordan into the Promised Land, naturally suggested a structure for this period. During this time, candidates for baptism were expected to make special progress under God's impulse. So too were the fully fledged members of the church community. Conversion is not a one-off job; like any life-long commitment, it will need to be renewed, perhaps several times. Where adult catechumens are to be received at Easter, we can all be powerfully stimulated to renewal as we accompany them on their journey to the fulness of faith. In this case, the readings for Year A, with their special reference to the baptimal themes of water, fresh vision and resurrection can be used on the 3rd, 4th and 5th Sundays.

The normal readings for this year lead to the climax of the Passion. Old Testament readings are linked to the events in Christ's life which they foreshadow, but which also speak to the condition of any Christian who takes baptism seriously. Like Christ, we shall be tempted. If we fail, we must repent like the prodigal son or the Samaritan woman. Paul provides a running commentary, and the epistle ties in with the themes of faith, light, reconciliation and resurrection in a way not usually possible during the rest of the year. The prayers complete the unity. With Christ tempted, we ask to understand the meaning of our belief in his Passion. We pray for enlightenment that will transfigure our lives, for confidence when discouraged in the face of our slow progress. We ask to be eager in following Christ's example. Overall, the mood is of confidence in God's action. In the words of the Lenten Preface, 'As we recall the great events that gave us a new life in Christ, you bring the image of your Son to perfection within us'.

Ash Wednesday

Today the Church summons us to conversion, to be seen not simply in external sacrifices, but rather in a true change of mind and heart.

First Reading   Joel 2: 12–18

The prophet sees in a plague of locusts a manifestation of the intervention of God in history to punish his people. As a result the oracle calls for sincere repentence. Priest and people are summoned to penance and prayer. However, the return to God must be more than merely external and cultic: 'Rend your hearts not your garments'. The command 'Return to me' (JB 'Come back') translates an Old Testament expression which is used of turning away from evil and turning to God. Thus it implies repentence and conversion. In the second part of the reading (vv. 15ff.) the priests are urged to call the people together to a service of national repentence. The form of the oracle is that of the 'national lament' (cf. p. 12).

Responsorial Psalm   51 (50)

℟ *Have mercy on us, O Lord, for we have sinned.*

1 Have mercy on me, God, in your kindness.
   In your compassion blot out my offence.
   O wash me more and more from my guilt
   and cleanse me from my sin. (R)

2 My offences truly I know them;
   my sin is always before me.
   Against you, you alone, have I sinned;
   what is evil in your sight I have done. (R)

3 A pure heart create for me, O God,
   put a steadfast spirit within me.
   Do not cast me away from your presence,
   nor deprive me of your holy spirit. (R)

4 Give me again the joy of your help;
   with a spirit of fervour sustain me,
   O Lord, open my lips
   and my mouth shall declare your praise. (R)

This best-known and most moving of the penitential Psalms is attributed to David; he acknowledges his sin of adultery. It was used very early in its history to express the penitence of the community. It is used in some Jewish rites for the Day of Atonement. Its dominant theme is fervent prayer for cleansing and renewal.

Second Reading   **2 Corinthians 5: 20–6: 2**

The theme of repentence and conversion continues in this reading in which St Paul calls for reconciliation with God. The Corinthians are called upon not to neglect the grace that has been given to them, 'for now is the acceptable time; now is the Day of Salvation'. The initiative of God in offering sinful man the means of reconciliation ought to be accepted, for the old creation has passed away and the new creation of Christ has come. The last verse of the reading is a quotation from Isaiah 49: 8, one of the Suffering Servant Songs where the Servant is assured of the certainty of God's help. Paul applies this to the present time, made 'acceptable' through the resurrection of Jesus Christ.

Gospel   **Matthew 6: 1–6, 16–18**

This reading is taken from the Sermon on the Mount, where the ideal for believers is set out. After the principles which guide the Christian's actions, examples are given of the practice of good works. True righteousness is urged as opposed to the spurious righteousness of the hypocrites. This true righteousness is illustrated by three examples characteristic of Jewish piety: almsgiving, prayer and fasting. A general principle is given first, followed by its particular applications. Each of these applications has the same structure. The closing verses return to the theme of good works being done 'in secret'; these, unlike those of the hypocrites, will involve a future reward from the Father.

First Sunday in Lent

The 'credo' of the Old Testament recited at the Passover Feast, and the 'credo' of the early Church mark the beginning of the Lenten

49

season which ends with the new Passover. The forty days Jesus spent in the wilderness have inspired the forty days of Lent.

First Reading **Deuteronomy 26: 4–10**

The ordinance of 'Moses' concerning the offering of the first-fruits and the liturgical ceremony to be used, is typical of the style of Deuteronomy, which sees the entry of the Israelites into the Promised Land as an event in the future. The recital of historical events which follows is often referred to as a cultic credo (similar recitals occur elsewhere e.g. Exodus 15: 1–18; Deuteronomy 6: 20–25; Joshua 24: 2–13). This declaration of faith and expression of gratitude transforms an old agricultural feast, since the offering made now is not to the rhythm of nature and a mere god of the harvest but to the God behind the historical events recalled in this 'credo'.

Responsorial Psalm **91 (90)**

℟ *Be with me, O Lord, in my distress.*

1 He who dwells in the shelter of the Most High
   and abides in the shade of the Almighty
   says to the Lord: 'My refuge,
   my stronghold, my God in whom I trust!' (R)

2 Upon you no evil shall fall,
   no plague approach where you dwell.
   For you has he commanded his angels,
   to keep you in all your ways. (R)

3 They shall bear you upon their hands
   lest you strike your foot against a stone.
   On the lion and the viper you will tread
   and trample the young lion and the dragon. (R)

4 His love he set on me, so I will rescue him;
   protect him for he knows my name.
   When he calls I shall answer: 'I am with you.'
   I will save him in distress and give him glory. (R)

This is a Psalm of trust (cf. Psalms of lament, p. 12) but with the intention of teaching (cf. wisdom Psalms). The Psalm does not make clear to whom the divine promise is addressed (vv. 2ff.); it does display the intimate relationship existing between the psalmist and God, as a result of which the prayer for help is answered.

Second Reading   **Romans 10: 8–13**

This reading from the letter to the Romans is taken from a longer section in which Paul speaks about Israel's exclusion from salvation as being through her own fault. In explaining Israel's fault Paul says that in the process of justification faith comes before outward profession. The exterior profession of faith and conformity of life should correspond to an interior disposition. But he goes on to state that faith of the heart alone is not sufficient either. What is demanded in the profession of faith is the *practice* of faith in everyday life. 'Lord' in verse 13 refers to Jesus Christ, and not Yahweh, as the context shows (it is a reference to Joel 2: 32, where 'Lord' refers to Yahweh). Thus in the formula of definition for a Christian, Christ is given the place ascribed to Yahweh in the definition of a Jew (cf. Acts 9: 14).

Gospel   **Luke 4: 1–13**

Before Jesus embarked on his public mission he retreated into the wilderness, no doubt to ponder its import. These forty days Jesus spent in the wilderness inspired the Lenten season. Luke agrees with Mark in saying that Jesus was tempted throughout these forty days. The three temptations recounted are the climax of the trial. The baptism episode which preceded this scene portrays Jesus as the Son of God commissioned for the messianic work of bringing mankind to the fulness of divine sonship. The temptation emphasizes that Jesus is also fully human. As man Jesus undertakes the work out of obedience. In his victory over temptation (v. 13) Jesus, as man, completes his role as Messiah, and conquers thus for every man. The full effects of this victory are to be seen in his public ministry. And in fact, all temptations are edited out of the public ministry by Luke, the evangelist who here anticipates the Passion, 'the appointed time' when the devil will return.

Second Sunday in Lent

Though it is God who initiates the covenant, man nevertheless has responsibilities which are necessary for his salvation. These are the conditions of discipleship imposed by Christ through whose death and resurrection we will share in the divine life.

First Reading   **Genesis 15: 5–12, 17–18**

Genesis 15 contains two stories. One describes a vision in which Abram is promised a great posterity. In spite of this seeming quite impossible (both he and his wife Sarai were old), Abram makes an act of faith in God, and thereby God accounts Abram 'just'. In Old Testament terminology 'justice' or 'righteousness' signifies a right relationship with God. Later Christian theology refers to this as sanctifying grace. The second story concerns the promise to Abram of the future possession of land. Central to this story are God's free gift and Abram's response in faith. The promise is solemnized in a covenant ritual. The fiery figures symbolize God (a common piece of symbolism in the Old Testament). In the ritual itself the passing between the parts of the animals symbolizes the willingness of the contracting parties to suffer the same fate if they break the covenant. Here only God passes between because the covenant is unilateral. In the New Covenant, later to be established, the initiative will again be taken by God.

Responsorial Psalm   27 (26)

℟ *The Lord is my light and my help.*

1 The Lord is my light and my help;
   whom shall I fear?
   The Lord is the stronghold of my life;
   before whom shall I shrink? (R)

2 O Lord, hear my voice when I call;
   have mercy and answer.
   Of you my heart has spoken:
   'Seek his face.' (R)

3 It is your face, O Lord, that I seek;
   hide not your face.

Dismiss not your servant in anger;
you have been my help. (R)

4 I am sure I shall see the Lord's goodness
in the land of the living.
Hope in him, hold firm and take heart.
Hope in the Lord! (R)

A Psalm of individual lament (cf. p. 12) containing the themes of trust and thanksgiving. The psalmist has set his prayer of distress in a context of reliance on God and contentment with his will.

Second Reading   **Philippians 3: 17–4: 1**

This section of Paul's letter is a warning against Jewish propaganda. The Judaizers under attack here may have been Christian Jews of the early Church who caused trouble among the Gentile communities of Paul's churches, by insisting that Gentile Christians should be circumcised and follow the Mosaic Law. Or they may simply have been non-Christian Jews. In stating the true way of salvation, Paul does not hesitate to propose himself as a model for their conduct. And he is a valid model because he himself imitates Christ (cf. 1 Corinthians 11: 1). He warns against those who glory in the obsolete dietary laws and circumcision rather than in the Cross of Christ. Christians have turned from such things. Union with Christ has transformed the Christian in a sense from the realm of earth to that of heaven, with the result that where Christ is so also is the Christian.

Gospel   **Luke 9: 28–36**

The account of the Transfiguration has been seen by some commentators as an Easter story read back into the public ministry. However, Peter's words in the story stand in the way of such an interpretation. In Luke the incident follows Jesus' teaching on the conditions of discipleship. The purpose of the heavenly revelation is to show that the Passion is something decreed by God. It serves also to corroborate Peter's profession of faith (Luke 9: 20), and is a way of strengthening the disciples for what lies ahead. Moses and Elijah represent the Law and the Prophets. The 'fear' of the disciples is due to their recognition of the Old Testament value of the cloud (the accompaniment of an appearance of God). The voice from heaven is reminiscent of the Baptism scene (Luke 3: 21–22), where Jesus was made aware of his mission. Here he is made aware of the full extent of his suffering and death: it is the way to glory and salvation.

Third Sunday in Lent

The life of the Israelites in the desert under the leadership of Moses is cited by Paul as an object lesson to Christians. We should never be complacent, but rather we should turn to God in true repentance.

First Reading   **Exodus 3: 1–8, 13–15**

The call of Moses was the prelude to the promise of God to deliver the people of Israel from the oppression of Pharaoh. The 'mountain of God' was probably an ancient cultic site. The 'angel of the Lord' is a circumlocution meaning God himself (cf. Genesis 16: 7, 13). It is common in the Old Testament for the presence of God to be signified by some spectacular natural phenomenon, such as the fire surrounding the bush in this instance. God first identifies himself and then declares his intention of saving his people. By this he demonstrates that he is a God involved in history; one who uses the events of history to achieve his purpose, and his own chosen servants (in this case Moses) to make known his intentions. It is in this passage (v. 14) that the divine name is first revealed.

Responsorial Psalm   **103 (102)**

℟ *The Lord is compassion and love.*

1 My soul, give thanks to the Lord,
  all my being, bless his holy name.
  My soul give thanks to the Lord
  and never forget all his blessing. (R)

2 It is he who forgives all your guilt,
  who heals every one of your ills,
  who redeems your life from the grave,
  who crowns you with love and compassion. (R)

3 The Lord does deeds of justice,
  gives judgement for all who are oppressed.
  He made known his ways to Moses
  and his deeds to Israel's sons. (R)

4 The Lord is compassion and love,
  slow to anger and rich in mercy.
  For as the heavens are high above the earth
  so strong is his love for those who fear him. (R)

A Psalm of thanksgiving (cf. p. 12), which could also be described as a hymn of praise. After acknowledging God's goodness the Psalm proceeds with a description of God's involvement with his people Israel, thus picking up the theme of the first reading.

Second Reading   **1 Corinthians 10: 1–6, 10–12**

Paul here takes up the Exodus theme, the event that followed God's promise to deliver the people of Israel from slavery in Egypt. Just as Moses led them across the Red (or Reed) Sea and followed the guiding cloud, so the new people of God follow Christ, united with him through baptism, of which the cloud and the crossing of the Sea are seen as types or prefigurements. These allusions to Israel's past are intended by Paul as lessons to the New Israel. The good things and bad which befell Israel under Moses should serve as a warning to the Christian that there is no room for complacency: 'Let anyone who thinks that he stands (i.e. is safe) take heed lest he fall'.

Gospel   **Luke 13: 1–9**

Today's reading is from a larger section (beginning at 12: 1) dealing with exhortation and warning. The passage itself concerns repentance and the consequence of failure to repent. Jesus uses the report of a tragic incident to underline the urgent need for Israel to repent before it is too late. He is neither condemning Pilate nor judging the Galileans. He further emphasizes the last chance that is being offered, by his parable of the fig-tree. The lesson that God is merciful and is ready to give the sinner another (and last) chance is symbolized by the digging around and manuring of the tree. Indeed, in Luke's Gospel as a whole the mercy of God is a central theme.

Fourth Sunday in Lent

Once again the themes of mercy and reconciliation dominate the readings. We are reminded also of the initiative of God 'who reconciled us to himself through Christ'.

First Reading   **Joshua 5: 9–12**

This account of the first Passover celebrated in the Promised Land seems to parallel the events recorded in Exodus 12. Just as the Israelites had celebrated the Passover on the day they left Egypt, so now they celebrate it when they enter the Promised Land. But the narrative also reports a turning-point of great significance for Israel: their period of wandering is now over. Indeed, the manna, symbol of that time of wandering in the wilderness, now ceases and they eat 'of the produce of the land', the symbol of settlement. The promise made to Abraham long ago has now been fulfilled and Israel has come into its inheritance. The Christian Passover of Easter recalls the inheritance of the New Israel, which is the promised land of the Kingdom of God.

Responsorial Psalm   34 (33)

℟ *Taste and see that the Lord is good.*

1 I will bless the Lord at all times,
   his praise always on my lips;
   in the Lord my soul shall make its boast.
   The humble shall hear and be glad. (R)

2 Glorify the Lord with me.
   Together let us praise his name.
   I sought the Lord and he answered me;
   from all my terrors he set me free. (R)

3 Look towards him and be radiant;
   let your faces not be abashed.
   This poor man called; the Lord heard him
   and rescued him from all his distress. (R)

This Psalm of thanksgiving (cf. p. 12) was perhaps composed by a teacher of wisdom in recognition of prayers having been answered.

From an initial thanksgiving the poem develops into an exhortation and invitation to faith.

Second Reading   **2 Corinthians 5: 17–21**

The redemptive activity of Christ has changed things radically. The old order is no more and the new order of creation has God as its source. In the New Covenant reconciliation with God is achieved through knowledge of and union with Jesus Christ, the risen Son of God whose life we now live. Thus Paul, as ambassador for God, exhorts us to allow the 'good news' of the gospel to have its effect, so that, in Christ, 'we might become the righteousness of God'.

Gospel   **Luke 15: 1–3, 11–32**

The theme of reconciliation continues here with the parable of the Prodigal Son. Indeed, the parable may well have been called the 'Prodigal Father', since the main character, the father, stands for God himself. His prodigality consists in his ever-readiness to forgive, without waiting for apology or explanation. Sufficient simply is the conversion and return of the sinner. The action of the younger son in recognizing his fault and going back to his father should encourage the sinner to repentance and reconciliation. The attitude of the elder son should not be overlooked since it, too, has a lesson for us. The (self-) righteous should not be jealous of the mercy that God extends to sinners. The passage is, in fact, taken from a longer section made up of three parables, all with the common theme of divine mercy. The essence of Luke's Gospel is here proclaimed: through Jesus Christ man is reconciled with God.

Fifth Sunday in Lent

Conversion and reconciliation mark not an end but a beginning. We should now forget the past and strive for what is still to come: 'the prize to which God calls us upwards to receive in Christ Jesus'.

First Reading   Isaiah 43: 16–21

This passage is taken from Second Isaiah (Isaiah 40–55), an anonymous prophet of the exilic period. It recounts one of his favourite themes: the new exodus. The prophet warns against glorying in the past that has no time for application in the present. The new exodus is a continuous act of redemption, brought about by the initiative of God. In spite of the ingratitude of the covenant people the steadfast love of God triumphs. In the context, the reference to deliverance is from the Babylonian exile, but at a deeper level it can be applied to deliverance from the exile of Satan and sin.

Responsorial Psalm   126 (125)

℟ *What marvels the Lord worked for us!*
  Indeed we were glad.

1 When the Lord delivered Zion from bondage,
  It seemed like a dream.
  Then was our mouth filled with laughter,
  on our lips there were songs. (℟)

2 The heathens themselves said: 'What marvels
  the Lord worked for them!'
  What marvels the Lord worked for us!
  Indeed we were glad. (℟)

3 Deliver us, O Lord, from our bondage
  as streams in dry land.
  Those who are sowing in tears
  will sing when they reap. (℟)

4 They go out, they go out, full of tears,
  carrying seed for the sowing:
  they come back, they come back, full of song,
  carrying their sheaves. (℟)

A Psalm of communal lament (cf. p. 12), possibly a prayer offered in the early years of the return from exile. The worshippers recall the salvation that was prayed for and promised. The restoration of fortunes has its fullest meaning in the reconciliation established by Christ.

Second Reading   **Philippians 3: 8–14**

Paul, in describing the 'gain' of his conversion, is explaining the gain of every Christian. When he speaks of 'knowing Christ Jesus', he is speaking, not of intellectual knowledge, but of that knowledge of experience which comes from communion with Christ. Thus the ultimate 'gain' will be the resurrection, when the final union with Christ will be attained. There is a certain urgency in Paul's striving. He likens himself to an athlete pressing on to capture the prize. And that prize, for Paul, is complete possession of Christ. He exhorts the Christian to do likewise. For it is the true destiny of the Christian to share a life with Christ in glory.

Gospel   **John 8: 1–11**

This passage recounts one of a number of incidents where the Scribes and Pharisees try to trap Jesus by their legalism and so find reason to condemn him. The penalty for adultery was death. The case is put specifically to Jesus: 'What have you to say?' If he was for mercy he would set himself against the Law of Moses; if he was for stoning to death he could be denounced to the Romans for murder. Jesus, however, refuses to treat the case simply as a legal matter and passes the problem back to his adversaries. They recognize the effectiveness of his reply and 'beginning with the eldest' (i.e., the most experienced) they depart. The lesson of the story is not that sin is unimportant, but rather that God extends mercy to the sinner who may, then, turn from sin and be saved.

HOLY WEEK

Liturgical Introduction

Jesus was put to death at Passover, and ever since, this season has been celebrated by Christians in his memory and at his command. Like the Jewish feast, Easter incorporates past, present and future. The past into which we are drawn extends back through Old Testament history to the deliverance from Egypt and beyond. The salvation from sin which the Exodus prefigured was won for us by Christ on the Cross, but it is still being worked out, and will only be complete at the end of time. This divine plan is massive in scope, embracing as it does the whole world. A concentrated overview allows each generation to relive the past and anticipate the future: it goes by the awkward name of the Paschal Mystery.

At first, Christians celebrated all these aspects of the Paschal Mystery in one great single feast – Exodus, Christ's death and resurrection, his ascension and the sending of the Holy Spirit. They even expected his second coming during the night of Easter. From the fourth century onwards, starting from the great pilgrimage centre of Jerusalem, the original feast was split up into the separate celebrations of Holy Week, Ascension, Whitsun and even Advent. This certainly allows us to enter more dramatically into the various phases of Christ's work, particularly the final moments of his earthly life. We need time to ponder the many facets presented on the successive days of Holy Week. Critics have pointed out possible dangers in this arrangement. Too much concentration on secondary ceremonies like the procession of palms, a tendency to dwell in a sentimental manner on Christ's sufferings, or worse, to separate suffering and death from the resurrection. However, the Easter Vigil preserves much of the original unity. A careful reading of the prayers of the liturgy also shows how they draw out the importance of each day without losing sight of the greater whole. In Lent, we might be tempted to think we were doing all the work. Holy Week and Whitsun remind us that the initiative rests firmly with God. It is in this frame of mind that we ponder on the successive phases of his creative and redemptive love, and then renew our baptismal promises in a mood of grateful joy for Christ's resurrection and ours.

Passion (Palm) Sunday

Readings now focus on Jesus as Messiah – not, however, the Messiah of popular belief, a great warrior-leader, but the humble Servant of the Lord who will give his life for the redemption of mankind.

Gospel of the Procession   **Luke 19: 28–40**

This passage, which recounts Jesus' triumphant entry into Jerusalem, is full of messianic overtones. The reference to the 'Mount of Olives' is not without significance, for Luke situates the important moments in Jesus' life on mountains (cf. also the Transfiguration, 9: 28; the Ascension, 24: 50; Acts 1: 12). The entry itself of Jesus as messianic King is a sign that the peace and salvation decreed by God is at hand. Significant is the use of an ass by Jesus to make his entry. Historically a prince coming to a city in peace would portray this fact symbolically by riding an ass and not a war-horse. The disciples recognize the significance of this gesture and respond by giving Jesus regal honours (though Luke omits the palm branches). Indeed, Luke, writing for Gentiles, modifies the idea of Kingdom (a Matthean theme) to that of King, and so concentrates on the *person* of Jesus. He also adds a couple of verses at the end (not found elsewhere) in which Jesus replies to some Pharisees with a proverb or prophecy, namely, that if the disciples do not proclaim him 'the very stones would cry out'.

First Reading   **Isaiah 50: 4–7**

The messianic theme of the procession reading is continued in this passage from Isaiah, which forms part of one of the Suffering Servant Songs. The Servant is speaking of his preaching mission and its difficulties, which here include personal violence. However, all is overcome by meekness and utter faith in God. The New Testament witnesses saw these songs to have had their fulfilment in Jesus, the

Messiah, who gave his own life that mankind might be reconciled with God.

Responsorial Psalm 22 (21)

℟ *My God, my God, why have you forsaken me?*

1 All who see me deride me.
   They curl their lips, they toss their heads.
   'He trusted in the Lord, let him save him;
   let him release him if this is his friend.' (R)

2 Many dogs have surrounded me,
   a band of the wicked beset me.
   They tear holes in my hands and my feet
   I can count every one of my bones. (R)

3 They divide my clothing among them.
   They cast lots for my robe.
   O Lord, do not leave me alone,
   my strength, make haste to help me! (R)

4 I will tell of your name to my brethren
   and praise you where they are assembled.
   'You who fear the Lord give him praise;
   all sons of Jacob, give him glory.
   Revere him, Israel's sons.' (R)

This Psalm combines an individual lament and thanksgiving (cf. p. 12), and echoes the sentiment of the preceding reading. Its opening verse was uttered by Jesus on the Cross (though Luke omits it in his account). It was not, however, uttered as a cry of despair, but as the beginning of a Psalm whose speaker has already experienced deliverance and who now offers (self-) sacrifice in return.

Second Reading Philippians 2: 6–11

These verses are seen as a hymn to Christ that proclaims the messianic paradox related in the gospel story. Christ the Son of God became man and accepted death as a ransom for man's sins. As a result he is exalted above all creation and takes his place at the head of his Kingdom, which is of heaven. Paul teaches nothing new in this passage on the divinity of Christ, nor is it his intention to do so. Rather the teaching is intended to exemplify from Christ's action the kind of mentality that should be found in a Christian. The Christian should be prepared to sacrifice his rights for the benefit of the community, just as Jesus did for the benefit of mankind.

Passion   **Luke 22: 14–23: 56**

The amount of space accorded to the Passion Narrative in the Gospels shows just how important it was held to be in the early Church. It was probably the first part of the gospel tradition to acquire a fixed structure. Each evangelist, however, has his own approach. Luke, while following Mark's to some extent, has arranged the order of events to give a clearer and smoother account. But, while seeking to set out well-ordered facts as in the work of any historian, he does not simply display a cold objectivity. His theological ideas (cf. p. 3) give a personal colouring to the account. He stresses the innocence of Jesus by omitting offensive and cruel details. In addition, the Passion is, for Luke, an appeal: the disciple, in turn, must follow Jesus on the way of the Cross. Also the major element in Luke's Gospel – forgiveness – is continued to the very end, with the pardoning of the thief.

Holy Thursday

Today's readings recall the establishment of the Passover of the Old Covenant, and the institution of the Eucharist, the Passover of the New Covenant.

First Reading   **Exodus 12: 1–8, 11–14**

This passage gives the general instructions for the celebration of the Passover. This feast was to become, in time, the most important in the Jewish liturgical calendar. It commemorated the angel of death's 'passing over' the homes of the Israelites in Egypt, as well as the Israelites' 'passing over' the Red Sea into freedom. It was during the Passover time that Jesus instituted the sacrament of the Eucharist.

In this case, however, the commemoration is not of a 'passing over' from earthly bondage, but a liberation from the slavery of sin and the dominion of Satan. In the new order the pascal sacrifice is not a lamb, but Jesus Christ, the Lamb who wrought our salvation.

Responsorial Psalm 116 (115)

℟ *The blessing-cup that we bless*
is a communion with the blood of Christ.

1 How can I repay the Lord
   for his goodness to me?
   The cup of salvation I will raise;
   I will call on the Lord's name. (R)

2 O precious in the eyes of the Lord
   is the death of his faithful.
   Your servant, Lord, your servant am I;
   you have loosened my bonds. (R)

3 A thanksgiving sacrifice I make:
   I will call on the Lord's name.
   My vows to the Lord I will fulfil
   before all his people. (R)

This Psalm of thanksgiving (cf. p. 12) sums up our attitude to God who has done for us such wonderful things. The Psalm's imagery of the 'cup of salvation' brings to mind the eucharistic cup left to us by Christ.

Second Reading 1 Corinthians 11: 23–26

In this passage Paul recalls the institution of the Eucharist which Jesus left us as his parting gift. The New Covenant, like the old one, is a pact made in blood, and, therefore, is marked by a sacrifice which is both the sign of the pact and the cause of it. 'This cup is the New Covenant in my blood' means that it is the blood of Christ which seals the New Covenant between God and man foretold in the Old Testament (Jeremiah 31: 31), and which is also the redeeming sacrifice that brought about man's reconciliation with God.

Gospel   **John 13: 1–15**

The actual account of the institution of the Eucharist is not recorded in John's Gospel. Instead John recounts Christ's discourse on the 'bread of life' (ch. 6). There are, however, several chapters dealing with the Last Supper and Jesus' final instructions to his disciples. In this reading Jesus instructs the disciples by way of example. The washing of their feet is Christ's way of teaching humility and brotherly love. The action has, in fact, two interpretations: baptismal (vv. 6–10), and moral (vv. 12–17). Each has its own conclusion: the first, 'you are clean . . .' (v. 10), that is, having been washed and purified by and in Christ; the second, 'Blessed are you . . .' (v. 17), that is, in doing to others as Christ did to you, you are blessed by them. Though the service of Maundy Thursday enacts the command of Christ literally, in fact any service of humble charity fulfils it.

Good Friday

In the liturgy commemorating our Lord's death, the readings concentrate on his humble acceptance of it for the sake of mankind. It was an acceptance of perfect obedience to the will of the Father. Acceptance brought death and, through death, victory.

First Reading   **Isaiah 52: 13–53: 12**

This reading consists of one of the Suffering Servant Songs. In this song the Servant of the Lord achieves victory and exaltation, paradoxically, through suffering. Indeed, this passage gives supreme expression to the doctrine of expiatory suffering. Through the suffering of one man salvation comes to all mankind. The New Testament writers identify Jesus as the Suffering Servant, and John sums up the public ministry of Christ in words taken from this very song. In the song we see the servant both at one with the people and yet distinct from them. His innocence separates him from his fellowmen and yet, in identifying himself with his brethren, his suffering becomes the atonement for all: 'through his wounds we are healed'.

Responsorial Psalm 31 (30)

℟ *Father, into your hands I commend my spirit.*

1 In you, O Lord, I take refuge.
  Let me never be put to shame.
  In your justice, set me free,
  Into your hands I commend my spirit.
  It is you who will redeem me, Lord. (R)

2 In the face of all my foes
  I am a reproach,
  an object of scorn to my neighbours
  and of fear to my friends. (R)

3 Those who see me in the street
  run far away from me.
  I am like a dead man, forgotten in men's hearts,
  like a thing thrown away. (R)

4 But as for me, I trust in you, Lord,
  I say: 'You are my God.'
  My life is in your hands, deliver me
  from the hands of those who hate me. (R)

5 Let your face shine on your servant.
  Save me in your love.
  Be strong, let your heart take courage,
  all who hope in the Lord. (R)

This is a Psalm of trust and thanksgiving uttered by one who has
been delivered from his afflictions. The sentiments pick up those of
the Servant in the preceding reading. The words of the response,
taken from the Psalm, and recorded by Luke, are those uttered by
Jesus himself at the moment of his redemptive death.

Second Reading Hebrews 4: 14–16; 5: 7–9

This passage is taken from a larger section dealing with the compassionate High Priest, Jesus, who is in sympathy with our miseries.
This compassion of Jesus should be to us a source of confidence.
Therefore we ought to turn to him in our need. In the final verses we
should see not only the Passion of Christ's humanity but also his
exaltation in glory. Because of this he was 'made perfect' and so

66

became a 'source (or cause) of eternal salvation' for all who obey him.

Passion   **John 18: 1–19: 42**

With the account of our Lord's Passion the goal of John's Gospel has
been reached. As in the other Gospels, the Passion Narrative plays a
large part in that of John. His account differs from those of the others
in that he makes it clear that the Passion is a victory, even though 'the
world' does not understand it as such. He does this by choosing his
material carefully. He gives no account of the agony in the garden.
The indignities suffered by Jesus at his trial are kept to a minimum.
On the other hand, because John is presenting Jesus as Lord of
Salvation, he brings out the Kingship of Jesus: when he speaks with
Pilate, and when he is crowned with thorns, it is as a king. Thus, for
John, the victory of Jesus is not only in his resurrection, but also in
his passion and death. Indeed, the whole 'passion, death and resurrection' event of Jesus is called by John his 'hour'. The achievement
of this 'hour' is recorded by the last words of Jesus on the Cross: 'It is
accomplished'. This is the 'hour' of Jesus' glorification: 'For this I
came into the world'.

Easter Vigil

'This is the night when Jesus Christ broke the chains of death and
rose triumphant from the grave' (Easter Proclamation).

Old Testament Readings

        Genesis 1: 1–2: 2
Psalm 104 (103): 1–2, 5–6, 10, 12–14, 24, 35
  or 33 (32): 4–7, 12–13, 20, 22
        Genesis 22: 1–18
Psalm 16 (15): 5, 8–11
        Exodus 14: 15–15: 1
Psalm Exodus 15: 1–7a, 17–18
        Isaiah 54: 5–14

Psalm 30 (29): 1–5, 10–12
       Isaiah 55: 1–11
Psalm Isaiah 12: 2–6
       Baruch 3: 9–15, 32–4: 4
Psalm 19 (18): 7–10
       Ezekiel 36: 16–17a, 18–28
Psalm 42 (41): 1–2, 4; 43 (42): 3–4
   or 51 (50): 10–13, 16–17

In the Scripture readings for the Vigil liturgy we have a summary of the history of salvation, from the creation of man to his restoration through the reconciliation with God brought about by the redemptive death of the risen Christ. The whole Christian mystery is to be seen in the vision presented by the Old Testament readings. In the beginning God created man 'in his own image and likeness', as the high point of his creation (Genesis 1). Even when, later, man turned away from God, the Creator continued to show him mercy and loving-kindness. But God also tested man, and when his servant Abraham proved his faith by obedience, God reckoned it to him as righteousness and made a covenant with him whereby the descendants of Abraham would be special to God (Genesis 22). God proved his own fidelity to the covenant he had made when he delivered the descendants of Abraham, his chosen people, from slavery in Egypt, of which the 'passing over' the Red Sea is a symbol and constant reminder (Exodus 14). This 'passing over' the Red Sea is the prefiguring of the Christian's 'passing through' the waters of baptism to be delivered from slavery to sin. However, whilst God showed himself faithful to the Covenant his chosen people did not. As a consequence they brought down judgement upon themselves, which resulted in their being taken from their 'promised land' to exile in Babylon. But God once more took pity on his people and brought them back from exile in what the prophet sees as a new exodus (Isaiah 54).

With this purified remnant of God's people a new covenant will be established (Isaiah 55) when God will, once more, bring them out of darkness into his light (Baruch 3). Their defilement will be washed away by God who will pour out clean water upon them and give them a new heart (Ezekiel 36).

All these saving events of God recounted in the Old Testament foreshadow the great redeeming act of Jesus Christ (foretold in Genesis 3), who, like Moses of old, has led the New Israel through the waters of baptism into the new life of the Spirit. This night's 'History of Salvation' explains the Christian mystery, which is the reconciliation of mankind with God through the redemption effected by Christ's death. The Easter sequence sums it up: 'The Paschal Victim . . . Christ the undefiled hath sinners to his Father reconciled'.

New Testament Reading   **Romans 6: 3–11**

Paul states that there is no more room for sin in the Christian life. He bases his argument for this on union with Christ, a union brought about by baptism. He demonstrates the nature of this union from the twofold baptismal ceremony of immersion and emersion. When the catechumen is *immersed* in the water he is being buried, as it were, with Christ, sharing his being dead to sin; when he *emerges* from the water he rises, as it were, with Christ from the tomb. Thus we learn from this passage the symbolism of the baptismal ceremony, the efficacy of the sacrament, and the effect of the sacrament, which is identification with Christ.

Responsorial Psalm   **118 (117)**

℟ *Alleluia, alleluia, alleluia!*

1 Alleluia!
Give thanks to the Lord for he is good,
for his love has no end.
Let the sons of Israel say:
'His love has no end.' (R)

2 The Lord's right hand has triumphed;
his right hand raised me up.
I shall not die, I shall live
and recount his deeds. (R)

3 The stone which the builders rejected
  has become the corner stone.
  This is the work of the Lord,
  a marvel in our eyes. (R)

This Psalm is a hymn of thanksgiving to God for all that he has done for his creatures. The corner-stone image was seen by New Testament writers to have had its fulfilment in Jesus Christ.

Gospel   **Luke 24: 1–12**

Luke differs from the other evangelists in that he sets the resurrection and the events which follow it all on one day, 'the first day of the week'. It is also the first day of the New Age – Sunday – which will displace the Sabbath of the old dispensation. Moreover all the appearances are recorded as having taken place in and around Jerusalem. This is because in Luke's plan Jerusalem is where the climax of his Gospel takes place (cf. p. 1). Luke has 'two men' delivering the news of Jesus' resurrection, but no command to go to Galilee (cf. Matthew and Mark). When the women returned with the news they were not believed. However, Peter 'ran to the tomb', found it to be as they had reported, and went back 'amazed at what had happened'. The light of faith begins to dawn.

EASTER

Easter Day

Today's readings are all concerned with the risen Christ and the new life of the Christian. 'Life's own champion slain, yet lives, to reign' (Easter Sequence).

First Reading   **Acts 10: 34, 37–43**

This passage is taken from Peter's classic discourse to the centurion Cornelius, the first Gentile convert. It summarizes the ministry of Jesus, appealing to eye-witness accounts. Peter goes on to say that the ministry of Jesus did not end with his death, because 'God raised him to life', a fact also testified to by eye-witnesses, of whom Peter himself was one. Those who were witnesses (Jesus did not appear to anybody and everybody) had the special commission of proclaiming Jesus risen from the dead, and appointed by God as universal Judge. The later written Gospels retain the general form of these early oral proclamations and expand them.

Responsorial Psalm   **118 (117)**

℟ *This day was made by the Lord; we rejoice and are glad.*
    or *Alleluia!*

1 Alleluia!
Give thanks to the Lord for he is good,
for his love has no end.
Let the sons of Israel say:
'His love has no end.' (R)

2 The Lord's right hand has triumphed;
his right hand raised me up.
I shall not die, I shall live
and recount his deeds. (R)

3 The stone which the builders rejected
has become the corner stone.
This is the work of the Lord,
a marvel in our eyes. (R)

This thanksgiving hymn (cf. p. 12) addressed to the whole community includes a victory song which uses the image of the rejected stone becoming the key-stone. Peter, when speaking before the Sanhedrin, applied this image directly to Jesus.

Second Reading   **Colossians 3: 1–4**

Set in their context, these verses are a positive counterpart to what precedes, where Paul is speaking out against false asceticism based on the 'principles of this world'. Unlike the 'child of this world' the Christian shares the life of the risen Christ here and now. Thus it is 'the things that are above' which should occupy the Christian (i.e., the things of ultimate concern rather than mere trivialities). Paul is attacking a materialistic type of superstition. In contrast he speaks of the life-giving union with Christ, which will one day be made obvious.

Alternative Second Reading   **1 Corinthians 5: 6–8**

Paul uses the metaphor of leaven for the corruptive influence of evil. It is a reference to the Jewish custom of destroying all leaven in preparation for the paschal feast during which only unleavened bread was allowed. He uses 'unleavened bread' as a symbol for those who are holy and pure. Hence the New Pasch is celebrated by 'getting rid of the yeast of evil and wickedness, having only the unleavened bread of sincerity and truth'. We see how Old Testament ceremonies were seen as types or prefigurements of Christ and life in the Church.

Gospel   **John 20: 1–9**

Nobody witnessed Jesus actually rise from the dead. The Gospel accounts, therefore, deal with the fact of the resurrection by testifying to the empty tomb of Easter morning and the subsequent appearances of the risen Jesus to his disciples. In John's account we hear how Peter and John, on hearing Mary Magdalene's news, go to the tomb to see for themselves. The mention of the burial clothes is probably to serve as visible evidence for the resurrection having taken place, and for the body not having been stolen. The disciples lead each other on, till both believe (John's reference to his own belief is not in contrast to Peter). Understanding dawns 'that Christ must rise from the dead'.

Second Sunday of Easter

The living Christ, once dead but now alive for ever, is present in our midst bringing healing and peace.

First reading   Acts 5: 12–16

After the resurrection the Christians became a distinctive group, drawn together by their common experience, though they still met in the Temple. At first they were respected by the rest of the community and were steadily winning converts. A noticeable feature of their activities was the continuing of Jesus' healing ministry. This was a period in the Church's history when God's power was revealed in this special way. There is a natural desire to have such signs of God's presence, but it is more important for us to realize that the Church's ministry of reconciliation and healing is continuous and not limited to special dramatic occasions.

Responsorial Psalm   118 (117)

℟ *Give thanks to the Lord for he is good,*
  for his love has no end.
  or *Alleluia!*

1 Let the sons of Israel say:
  'His love has no end.'
  Let the sons of Aaron say:
  'His love has no end.'
  Let those who fear the Lord say:
  'His love has no end.' (R)

2 The stone which the builders rejected
  has become the corner stone.
  This is the work of the Lord,
  a marvel in our eyes.
  This day was made by the Lord;
  we rejoice and are glad. (R)

3 O Lord, grant us salvation;
   O Lord, grant success.
   Blessed in the name of the Lord
   is he who comes.
   We bless you from the house of the Lord;
   the Lord God is our light. (R)

A Psalm of thanksgiving (cf. p. 12), probably part of a liturgy for the procession to the Temple on a great feast. Jesus claimed that he was 'the stone which the builders rejected'.

Second Reading   **Revelation (Apocalypse) 1: 9–13, 17–19**

The Apocalypse is a fascinating book with its vivid poetic imagery and dramatic confrontations between the forces of good and evil. It was probably written towards the end of the first century AD, when Domitian tried to force the Christians to worship him, the emperor, as divine. This passage tells of the call of the author, John, to write the book. He was probably a prisoner in the convict settlement on the isle of Patmos at the time. His overall purpose seems to have been to warn the Christians that they too would soon face persecution for their faith and to encourage them to stand firm and remain faithful. John saw Christ in the form of the Son of Man in Daniel (another apocalyptic book addressed to people facing persecution). Christ was standing in the middle of seven golden candlesticks, representing the seven churches of Asia, master of death and the underworld, so he could reassure John.

Gospel   **John 20: 19–31**

This Gospel has a special message for those who, like ourselves, hear the good news of the resurrection through others. Thomas was missing on the evening of Easter Day when the other disciples saw Jesus in their midst and were commissioned to continue his work. He did not believe them when they told him what had happened. He seems to have been cautious and inclined to look on the dark side. Previously when Jesus, hearing of the death of Lazarus, had declared his intention of going to Bethany, although the Jews were threatening to stone him, Thomas had said, 'Let us also go that we may die with him . . .' – showing his courage and loyalty as well as his pessimism. When a week after the resurrection Jesus again appeared and offered Thomas the tangible proofs he had demanded, his doubts were resolved. Jesus then commended those in the future who would 'not have seen and yet believe'.

Third Sunday of Easter

'Christ is Lord', declared the apostles and refused to be silenced, even by imprisonment and flogging.

First Reading   **Acts 5: 27–32, 40–41**

Not long after the Resurrection opposition began to grow against the Christians. Their claim that Jesus had been raised from the dead was particularly unacceptable to the Sadducees, who did not believe in resurrection. This reading comes from an account of one of the clashes between Christians and Sadducees. The apostles had been arrested and imprisoned. When they appeared in court the high priest accused them of making the Jewish Council responsible for the death of Jesus. The apostles' answer so angered the Council that it considered sentencing them to death. However Gamaliel, a leading Pharisee, spoke against it, for the Pharisees believed there was a resurrection. It was decided to flog the apostles and set them free with a warning to stop their preaching. The apostles ignored it, 'glad to have the honour of suffering humiliation for the sake of the name'.

Responsorial Psalm   **30 (29)**

℟ *I will praise you, Lord,*
you have rescued me.
or *Alleluia!*

1 I will praise you, Lord, you have rescued me
and have not let my enemies rejoice over me.
O Lord, you have raised my soul from the dead,
restored me to life from those who sink into the grave. (℟)

2 Sing psalms to the Lord, you who love him,
give thanks to his holy name.

His anger lasts but a moment; his favour through life.
At night there are tears, but joy comes with dawn. (R)

3 The Lord listened and had pity.
The Lord came to my help.
For me you have changed my mourning into dancing,
O Lord my God, I will thank you for ever. (R)

A Psalm of thanksgiving for deliverance from death, used at the Jewish Feast of Dedication. This commemorated the restoration of worship in the Temple in 165 BC after its desecration by the Syrians, and the deliverance of the Jews from persecution.

Second Reading   **Revelation (Apocalypse) 5: 11–14**

Here John saw the risen Christ in the form of 'a Lamb that had been sacrificed', and was now exalted beside God and worshipped with him, not only by the host of heaven but by all creation. Like so much of this puzzling book, the description is vivid and fires the imagination, even when difficult to understand. This is one of several glimpses of the worship of God in heaven, which provides the constant background of the whole book, against which are set the sufferings and persecutions that will afflict those on earth before the glorious and final end. The persecuted are reminded that their sufferings are transitory and are only one aspect of the scene. After a brief spell they too will join the worshipping hosts of heaven.

Gospel   **John 21: 1–19**

This account of Jesus' appearance to apostles fishing in the Sea of Tiberias is only found in the Fourth Gospel, in an appendix to the Gospel (which originally ended with ch. 20). A common feature of several of the accounts of Christ's resurrection appearances is the failure of those who saw him to recognize him at first. This was not because of anything supernatural in his appearance, for he was mistaken for a gardener, or a fellow-traveller. Here he was recognized by Peter as a result of the large catch of fish following a night of failure. After they have breakfasted together Peter is given the chance to redeem his threefold denial with a threefold affirmation of his love.

Fourth Sunday of Easter

Jesus the Lamb – once slain, now glorified – is also the good shepherd whom the prophets had foretold God would send.

First Reading   **Acts 13: 14, 43–52**

When Paul and Barnabas visited Perga, they went to the synagogue on the sabbath and were invited to speak after the reading of the Law. They used the opportunity to show how Jesus had fulfilled the promise of the prophets and yet had been rejected and condemned to death by his own people. However, God had vindicated him, raising him from the dead so that all might receive forgiveness of their sins. The congregation, impressed, asked Paul and Barnabas to return the next week. When many Gentiles also came, the Jews opposed the teaching. This Jewish opposition was so violent that the apostles had to leave the city, declaring that their instructions from God were now to preach to the Gentiles.

Responsorial Psalm   **100 (99)**

℞ *We are his people, the sheep of his flock.*
   or *Alleluia!*

1 Cry out with joy to the Lord, all the earth.
  Serve the Lord with gladness.
  Come before him, singing for joy. (R)

2 Know that he, the Lord, is God.
  He made us, we belong to him,
  we are his people, the sheep of his flock. (R)

3 Indeed, how good is the Lord,
  eternal his merciful love.
  He is faithful from age to age. (R)

A processional hymn which was probably used as an introit on entering the Temple. It summarizes our faith in God as our Lord and creator, whose merciful love constantly watches over us.

Second Reading   **Revelation (Apocalypse) 7: 9, 14–17**

John saw worshipping in heaven a vast host of people from every race, nation and language united by their past suffering and their redemption in Christ. Their sufferings are at an end because the Lamb has now become their shepherd. 'Shepherd' is often used of kings and leaders, both good and bad. After the humiliation of the capture of Jerusalem by the Babylonians Ezekiel (ch. 34) had slated the Jewish leaders as bad shepherds whose greed and indifference to their responsibilities had led to the catastrophe. He promised that God himself would be his people's good shepherd. Here this is seen to be Christ.

Gospel   **John 10: 27–30**

In this chapter the teaching about good and bad shepherds is further developed. First comes the warning about the thief who is only concerned about his own interests; and then about the hired shepherd, who runs away to save his own skin. By contrast, Jesus, the good shepherd, protects the flock committed to him by his Father at the expense of his own life. The occasion of this teaching was the Feast of Dedication commemorating the purification of the Temple after it had been defiled by the Syrians. The Jews had gathered round Jesus and demanded a straight answer to the question: 'Are you the Messiah?' He answered that the question was unnecessary. It had already been answered but they were not prepared to accept it, in contrast to those who belonged to his flock, who had recognized him, who listened and followed him, secure in the care of the Father.

Fifth Sunday of Easter

Christ gives us his new commandment to love one another and encourages us with the promise of the new Jerusalem.

First Reading   **Acts 14: 21–27**

Paul and Barnabas were forced to leave Antioch in Pisidia because of the opposition of the Jews. They travelled on, still pursued by the hostility of the Jews. Then they decided to return to their base in Syrian Antioch. On the way they revisited the towns where they had preached, to encourage their converts and to organize the local churches they had established. When they reached Syrian Antioch, the place of their original commissioning, they reported on what they had done, and on their success in preaching the Christian message to the Gentiles.

Responsorial Psalm 145 (144)

℟ *I will bless your name for ever, O God, my King.*
   or *Alleluia!*

1 The Lord is kind and full of compassion,
   slow to anger, abounding in love.
   How good is the Lord to all,
   compassionate to all his creatures. (R)

2 All your creatures shall thank you, O Lord,
   and your friends shall repeat their blessing.
   They shall speak of the glory of your reign
   and declare your might, O God,
   to make known to men your mighty deeds
   and the glorious splendour of your reign. (R)

3 Yours is an everlasting kingdom;
   your rule lasts from age to age. (R)

One of the alphabetical Psalms (cf. p. 13). The responsorial verse emphasizes 'bless', one of the key words of the Psalm, which tells of God's compassion.

Second Reading **Revelation (Apocalypse) 21: 1–5**

John here describes his final vision. The old earth has disappeared and with it the sea, and is replaced by the new Jerusalem, beautiful as a bride on her wedding day. The source of her beauty is God's presence in her as he comes to live with his people and be their God. The promises made through the prophets are thus fulfilled. The words 'his name is God-with-them' recall the prophecy in Isaiah (ch. 7) about the child who is to be called Immanuel (God-with-us).

Gospel **John 13: 31–35**

We tend to take it for granted that Jesus told us to love one another, without bothering about the occasion on which he did this. It comes as a shock to realize that the setting was immediately after Judas had left the upper room to go to betray Jesus to his enemies. Jesus was not only aware of what Judas was going to do but spoke of its consequences as his glorification. This is the only place in this Gospel where the form of address 'little children' is used, but the phrase occurs several times in the first epistle of John. This and the emphasis on the command to love one another link the two books together. The command to love is without limit. Like the love of Jesus himself ('just as I have loved you') it is to include everyone, even Judas. This was the new commandment he had come to bring and the sign by which the world would recognize his followers.

Sixth Sunday of Easter

The early Christians rejoiced in the presence of the Holy Spirit in their midst and trusted him to guide them in all their decisions.

First Reading **Acts 15: 1–2, 22–29**

Paul and Barnabas in preaching to the Gentiles had sparked off a controversy about what made a Christian. Was baptism in the name of Jesus sufficient? Or must Gentile Christians be circumcised and keep all the Jewish Law? It was decided that this was too important a question to be settled locally, so Paul and Barnabas were sent to Jerusalem to consult the Apostles. The Church met in Council and Peter told how he had been commanded in a vision to visit the Gentile Cornelius and how while he was preaching to him, the Holy Spirit had fallen on all his household, showing that Gentiles too were acceptable to God. So he baptized them. The Council accepted this and sent word back to Antioch that Gentiles need not be circumcised, but were expected to renounce idolatry and immoral behaviour, and to accept a minimum of ritual requirements which would make 'table fellowship' between Jewish and Gentile Christians possible.

Responsorial Psalm 67 (66)

℞ *Let the peoples praise you, O God;*
  let all the peoples praise you.
  or *Alleluia!*

1 O God, be gracious and bless us
  and let your face shed its light upon us.
  So will your ways be known upon earth
  and all nations learn your saving help. (R)

2 Let the nations be glad and exult
  for you rule the world with justice.
  With fairness you rule the peoples.
  you guide the nations on earth. (R)

3 Let the peoples praise you, O God;
  let all the peoples praise you.
  May God still give us his blessing
  till the ends of the earth revere him. (R)

These verses come from a Psalm of thanksgiving used in the harvest festival. The emphasis throughout is on the Giver rather than on his gifts.

Second Reading   **Revelation (Apocalypse) 21: 10–14, 22–23**

John was now taken to see the new Jerusalem which he had glimpsed before. Its light was the radiant glory of God, which made all other forms of light unnecessary. It was more brilliant than the glory which had filled Solomon's Temple at its dedication so powerfully that the priests had been unable to remain there. The only earthly thing with which he can compare it is the brilliance of precious jewels. In the earthly city the Temple had marked the place where God dwelt among his people; in the new Jerusalem there was no temple because God and Christ were fully present there in all their glory.

Gospel   **John 14: 23–29**

In the Fourth Gospel the account of the Last Supper consists chiefly of Jesus talking to his disciples, preparing them for what is to come.

They were obviously anxious and fearful; Peter had volunteered to follow Jesus even if it meant death. But Jesus realized that their questions and Peter's too-ready offer to die with him only showed that they still failed to realize who he was. After repeating the commandment that they should love one another, he comforted them by promising that the Father would send the Holy Spirit, the advocate who would speak for him and remind them of his teaching.

Ascension Day

Christ ascends to glory in heaven giving us the hope that we shall one day follow him there.

First Reading   **Acts 1: 1–11**

These opening words of Luke's 'Acts' take up the theme of the end of his Gospel, the last of the resurrection appearances to the disciples. In both books Luke concentrates the events of the post-resurrection period in and around Jerusalem, though the other Gospels know a tradition of appearances in Galilee. This occasion had a finality about it which provoked the disciples' question whether the kingdom was now to be restored to Israel. Instead of answering, Jesus pointed to the work ahead for which the Spirit would give them power. As he spoke 'he was lifted up'. This spatial imagery offends some people, but even the most literal-minded use metaphorical language at times (e.g., 'down-hearted'). Some experiences can only be expressed in such imagery. This is one.

Responsorial Psalm   **47 (46)**

℟ *God goes up with shouts of joy;*
  the Lord goes up with trumpet blast.
  or *Alleluia!*

1 All peoples, clap your hands,
  cry to God with shouts of joy!
  For the Lord, the Most High, we must fear,
  great king over all the earth. (R)

2 God goes up with shouts of joy;
   the Lord goes up with trumpet blast
   Sing praise for God, sing praise,
   sing praise to our king, sing praise. (R)

3 God is king of all the earth.
   Sing praise with all your skill.
   God is king over the nations;
   God reigns on his holy throne. (R)

Some link this Psalm with an annual festival when the Ark of the Covenant was taken in procession into the Temple as a sign of God's victorious entry and enthronement over Israel.

Second Reading   **Ephesians 1: 17–23**

The theme of this passage is the exaltation of Jesus and the hope and security that this brings us. From the first Jesus was seen as 'victor' over all the spirits of good and evil in which people in those days believed. The writer declares that Christ is 'far above every Sovereignty, Authority, Power or Domination, or any other name that can be named, not only in this age but also in the age to come'. Nothing and no one is able to withstand him. His power is 'exercised for us believers'. This is the theme of today's celebration into which we are invited to enter.

Gospel   **Luke 24: 46–53**

These closing words of Luke's Gospel were taken up by today's first reading from the Acts. This account is briefer and does not mention the 'cloud' or 'two men in white' or the promise of Christ's return 'in the same way as you have seen him go'. But the Holy Spirit is promised, to bring them power to witness to the resurrection. It is also significant that the disciples 'were full of joy' even though Jesus had withdrawn from them. This account names the place where the Ascension took place as Bethany, on the far side from Jerusalem of the Mount of Olives.

Seventh Sunday of Easter

Love unites all believers with God and so with one another.

First Reading   **Acts 7: 55–60**

The readings from Acts selected for this period do not follow in chronological order. This passage comes from the account of the early days of the Church. As numbers grew, the apostles found that they needed help in the daily distribution of food to the poor so seven helpers were appointed for them. Stephen was one of these but he soon became known for his forceful preaching of the Christian message. He was brought before the high priest and there accused the Jewish Council of murdering the Righteous One, whom God had sent to them. His hearers were so angry at this that they rushed at him, flung him out of the city and stoned him to death. Stephen thus became the first martyr for Christ. Like Jesus he prayed for the forgiveness of those who were killing him. We find here the earliest reference to Paul (here called Saul). He took an official part in the execution, probably representing the Rabbis.

Responsorial Psalm   **97 (96)**

℟ *The Lord is king, most high above all the earth.*
or *Alleluia!*

1 The Lord is king, let earth rejoice,
   the many coastlands be glad.
   His throne is justice and right. (R)

2 The skies proclaim his justice;
   all peoples see his glory.
   All you spirits, worship him. (R)

3 For you indeed are the Lord
   most high above all the earth
   exalted far above all spirits. (R)

This is one of a group of six Psalms which proclaim God's kingship over all the earth.

Second Reading   **Revelation (Apocalypse) 22: 12–14, 16–17, 20**

The Apocalypse, and so the Bible, closes with these words. John is told that the promises which have been given him will soon be fulfilled. Alpha and Omega are the first and last letters of the Greek alphabet and used together, as here, they stand for totality or completeness. This is also the meaning here of First and Last, Beginning and Ending. The threefold repetition emphasizes the completeness of Christ. 'The Spirit' here stands for the prophets and 'the Bride' for the Saints, who are all united in praying Jesus to come and satisfy the needs of all. Jesus himself is the guarantor of the truth of the revelation given to John and promises to come soon. Amen; come, Lord Jesus.

Gospel   **John 17: 20–26**

The great 'high-priestly prayer' of Jesus is placed at the end of the Last Supper in the Fourth Gospel. The prayer begins by calling on the Father to glorify the Son who has now carried out the work he was given to do on earth. Then comes prayer for the disciples whom God has given to the care of the Son, and who, up to that point, have been protected by his presence, while being taught what he has learned from the Father. Now they are to be sent out into the world to carry on with his work. The section which forms today's Gospel is the prayer for us: 'those also who through their words put their faith in me'. Our union with the Father and the Son and so with one another is to be as close as is the union between the Father and the Son. Our Lord wants us to be with him and to see his glory, he and we together revealing God's love to those whom the Father has given him down the ages.

Pentecost Sunday

Christ's Church is filled with the power of the Holy Spirit.

First Reading   **Acts 2: 1–11**

The day of Pentecost was one of the three major Jewish feasts, a harvest festival of the first fruits of the grain harvest. At some period this festival also became associated with the making of the covenant on Mount Sinai. The twelve in the upper room experienced the traditional, Old Testament signs of the presence of God: wind and fire. In addition the apostles were given the power of ecstatic utterance in a variety of languages which were recognized by the Jews of the dispersion there as the languages of the countries where they normally lived. There is no mention that these bystanders saw the fire or heard the wind, but the 'speaking with tongues' made them aware that something unusual was taking place.

Responsorial Psalm   104 (103)

℟ *Send forth your Spirit, O Lord,*
  and renew the face of the earth.
  or *Alleluia!*

1 Bless the Lord, my soul!
  Lord God, how great you are,
  How many are your works, O Lord!
  The earth is full of your riches. (R)

2 You take back your spirit, they die,
  returning to the dust from which they came.
  You send forth your spirit, they are created;
  and you renew the face of the earth. (R)

3 May the glory of the Lord last for ever!
  May the Lord rejoice in his works!
  May my thoughts be pleasing to him.
  I find my joy in the Lord. (R)

This hymn opens with a vision of God 'wrapped in light as a robe'. God is praised not only as creator but as the One who by the Spirit will give new and full life to all.

Second Reading   1 Corinthians 12: 3–7, 12–13

When Paul speaks about the gifts of the Spirit, foremost among them is the power to recognize Jesus as Lord. But Paul saw the Christian community as Christ's Body . . . Do we acknowledge one another? Just as the human body needs all its many parts for efficient functioning and health, so the Church needs all the different individuals with their wide variety of gifts and abilities provided by the Holy Spirit. All are made into one body by baptism, regardless of differences of nationality, culture and social position. All are needed; all have their part to play.

Gospel **John 20: 19–23**

It is well known that this Gospel presents the ministry and teaching of Jesus differently from the other Gospels. Some events are omitted and their significance indicated in other ways. So here on Easter Day the appearance of the risen Christ to his disciples in the upper room is also made the occasion of their being commissioned to carry on his work of reconciliation through the gift of the Holy Spirit. The day of Christ's resurrection is seen as the day of his glorification and ascension to the Father: a different emphasis from that in Luke.

Trinity Sunday

Glory to God: the Father, the Son and the Holy Spirit.

First Reading **Proverbs 8: 22–31**

There are passages in the Old Testament where the trinitarian idea of God is anticipated. One important group of such passages are those describing the Wisdom of God, in books that are known as the Wisdom literature. This passage from Proverbs is one of the most outstanding of these. In it God's Wisdom is seen as almost having a separate identity from God himself. Wisdom is associated with God in the act of creation, being 'by his side, a master craftsman' as this passage puts it. These passages may have been the source of the doctrine of the pre-existence of Christ from before creation as we see it developed in the epistles. They describe vividly the fellowship and common purpose of the Father and the Son.

Responsorial Psalm　　　　　　　　　　　　　　　　8

℟ *How great is your name, O Lord our God,*
through all the earth!

1　When I see the heavens, the work of your hands,
　the moon and the stars which you arranged,
　what is man that you should keep him in mind,
　mortal man that you care for him? (R)

2　Yet you have made him little less than a god;
　with glory and honour you crowned him,
　gave him power over the works of your hand,
　put all things under his feet. (R)

3　All of them, sheep and cattle,
　yes, even the savage beasts,
　birds of the air, and fish
　that make their way through the waters. (R)

This is a hymn on the theme of the majesty of God as revealed in his creation, and the dignity of man, because he too is created by God.

Second Reading　　　　　　　　　　　　　　**Romans 5: 1–5**

Paul, like a good Jew, has been explaining to his readers how Abraham has his place in the Christian scheme and that he is 'the father of us all', both Gentile and Jew, because it was through his faith that he had been found acceptable to God. Paul then described in these verses the heart of the Christian experience as 'peace with God' 'since it is by faith and through Jesus that we have entered into this state of grace'. The relationship involved all the Persons of the Trinity: 'peace with God', 'through Jesus', and with the love of God 'poured into our hearts by the Holy Spirit'. The doctrine of the Trinity was not a dogmatic statement for Paul but the only adequate way he could describe his own experience and that of his converts.

Gospel　　　　　　　　　　　　　　　　　**John 16: 12–15**

Jesus has just warned his disciples of future persecution and promised them the Spirit of truth. Here he faces the inability of the disciples to understand what he is saying to them. He promises that the coming of the Advocate will give them a second chance to understand, when they are more able to take in the message. After the test which lies immediately ahead of the disciples, there will come the time when 'their grief will be turned into joy'. Then they will remember and understand.

Note on Sundays in Ordinary Time

The first Sunday in Ordinary Time is always the feast of the Baptism of the Lord. The other Sundays then follow until Lent supervenes; the sequence begins again on the Sunday after Trinity Sunday. However, the sequence does not recommence exactly where it left off. (This gives the flexibility essential because years vary in their number of Sundays and in the position of Easter.) Either two or three Sundays are omitted in any one year. The table shows which these will be.

Sundays in Ordinary Time

Years	5	6	7	8	9	10	11	12
1983	6 Feb	13 Feb	—	—	—	5 Jun	12 Jun	19 Jun
1986	9 Feb	—	—	—	1 Jun	8 Jun	15 Jun	22 Jun
1989	5 Feb	—	—	28 May	4 Jun	11 Jun	18 Jun	25 Jun
1992	11 Feb	18 Feb	25 Feb	3 Mar	—	—	—	21 Jun
1995	5 Feb	12 Feb	19 Feb	26 Feb	—	—	18 Jun	25 Jun

Ordinary Time

Second Sunday in Ordinary Time

God rescues his own, he is good to them, he gives them his Spirit (the 'new wine' of his saving love). That is the gospel, the 'good news', which men may hear and in which they may rejoice.

First Reading   Isaiah 62: 1–5

This passage probably dates from the Exile. The prophet expresses his determination to persevere in his 'optimistic' promise of a future deliverance when Israel's misfortunes would be reversed. This optimism (for which the prophet had probably already been derided by his fellows) was not based on a merely secular hopefulness (the idea that 'nothing is as bad as it seems' or that 'every cloud has a silver lining'), but rather on the covenant-keeping faithfulness of God. Isaiah's message is that the day *will* come when the seemingly forsaken ones will discover the abiding and intimate presence of their Lord.

Responsorial Psalm   **96 (95)**

℟ *Proclaim the wonders of the Lord*
among all the peoples.

1 O sing a new song to the Lord,
   sing to the Lord all the earth.
   O sing to the Lord, bless his name. (R)

2 Proclaim his help day by day,
   tell among the nations his glory
   and his wonders among all the peoples. (R)

3 Give the Lord, you families of peoples,
   give the Lord glory and power,
   give the Lord the glory of his name. (R)

4 Worship the Lord in his temple.
   O earth, tremble before him.
   Proclaim to the nations: 'God is king.'
   He will judge the peoples in fairness. (R)

A hymn of thanksgiving (cf. p. 12), praising God for his deliverance of his people from some oppression. God has manifested his lordship in the deliverance of Israel from Egypt, in his restoration of Israel after the Exile – and, from our viewpoint, in that greater deliverance of men through the cross and resurrection of Jesus. Worship always involves this glad thankfulness, because worship re-affirms that God, the king, is for us and with us.

Second Reading   **1 Corinthians 12: 4–11**

Paul's underlying conviction is that God has kept faith and has fulfilled his promises to Israel. Through his Spirit, men today can enjoy intimate relationship with God (cf. Galatians 4: 6). This same Spirit works within the life of the Church, sustaining it and creating within it possibilities of enrichment, worship and outreach. Paul maintains that the Church is always a 'charismatic' community, that is to say one that lives by the 'charismata' (meaning 'gifts') imparted to men by this dynamic Spirit, the creative breath of God himself. God's Spirit is not divisive: wherever he works, he strives for the upbuilding of the total community. Differences within corporate life can become occasions for faction; yet, properly grasped, it is precisely variety that can promote growth and development.

Gospel   **John 2: 1–12**

The Fourth Gospel places this astonishing miracle (consider the quantity of wine, and this after men had well drunk!) at the outset of Jesus' ministry. It highlights the dramatic renewal of God's people brought about through the life, death and resurrection of Jesus. The flat, anaemic water of Judaism is transformed into the rich and heady wine of the gospel and of the gospel community. (The same point, though with its negative aspect foremost, is made in the story of the cleansing of the Temple which, in John's Gospel, is brought forward to the start of Jesus' public ministry (contrast Mark 11: 15–19) and follows immediately the Cana miracle.) Jesus' retort to his mother (v. 4) reminds us that this transformation of ordinary water into wine is only an anticipation (only a parable) of the real act of redemption and re-creation which occurs when, at last, his 'time' *has* come (see John 12: 23ff., 17: 1).

Third Sunday in Ordinary Time

Last Sunday's readings were about rejoicing in God's good and redemptive work; this Sunday's theme is the proclamation of that work. The Church's task is to make known to all and sundry that there *is* a God in heaven and that this God *cares* about the world that he has made.

First Reading   **Nehemiah 8: 2–6, 8–10**

We are in the time shortly before 400 BC. The Exile in Babylon is over, Ezra and Nehemiah have contributed to the restoration of basic political and religious life in Jerusalem, and the damaged walls of that city have at last been made good despite many hindrances on the part of indigenous peoples. This basic work completed, we now read of Ezra's public proclamation of God's Law. The compiler of Nehemiah sees it as appropriate to juxtapose the completing of the walls of Jerusalem and the proclamation of God's word; for of what value is a fortified city unless God is honoured and known within its walls? The proclamation is such that people hear and understand (maybe verse 8 means that the Law was read in Hebrew and then translated into Aramaic, the common tongue of that time), and understanding leads to the response of penitence and worship.

Responsorial Psalm   **19 (18)**

℟ *Your words are spirit, Lord,*
 and they are life.

1 The law of the Lord is perfect,
  it revives the soul.
  The rule of the Lord is to be trusted,
  it gives wisdom to the simple. (R)

2 The precepts of the Lord are right,
  they gladden the heart.
  The command of the Lord is clear,
  it gives light to the eyes. (R)

3 The fear of the Lord is holy,
  abiding for ever.
  The decrees of the Lord are truth
  and all of them just. (R)

4 May the spoken words of my mouth,
  the thoughts of my heart,
  win favour in your sight, O Lord,
  my rescuer, my rock! (R)

This Psalm combines two themes (not infrequently related in the Old Testament): the glory of God manifest in the natural order of the world, and the graciousness of God revealed in his Law. It is this second theme on which our verses concentrate. The Law is not a heavy burden for men to shoulder but the glad provision by God of guidance and succour.

Second Reading   1 Corinthians 12: 12–30

The old community which bowed and wept before the Law, is now the renewed community, revived by the saving events of Jesus' ministry and by the outpoured Spirit. Paul here likens this community to a body in which each part has its proper function. Not every part has the same function, of course! But each part with its assigned task contributes to the well-being of the whole. God's Spirit is not imposing upon God's people a dull uniformity; quite the reverse, he inculcates a rich and enriching variety. Within this full variety, through love, unity is to be found and expressed. This 'body' works and exists not for its own sake, but as a vehicle of Christ, who is himself active in and through it (v. 27).

Gospel   Luke 1: 1–4, 4:14–21

The Mosaic Law consisted not only in teaching but in the record of what God had done for his people. Likewise the Gospel contains not only sayings of Jesus, but the story of his living, dying and rising, for it was in these events that God accomplished his saving plan for mankind. Therefore it is not a matter of indifference how accurate the record of these events is. Luke testifies that he has taken great care to check his sources and to give us, to the best of his knowledge, an account of what *actually happened;* not indeed, for the mere sake of it, but to elicit from his readers a response ('that you may know', v. 4). This account concerns him who was himself the fulfiller and fulfilment of the Old Testament hopes; so, when Ezra read the Law, people attended to *it*, but when Jesus read from the Old Testament 'the eyes of all were fixed upon *him*' (v. 21).

Fourth Sunday in Ordinary Time

'Love bears all things . . . endures all things' (1 Corinthians 13: 7). God is sovereign and loving; to be in his hand is to be safe and sound. Yet his love for us does not relieve us of the necessity of suffering – rather, it enables us to endure. God does not save us *from* suffering but leads and accompanies us *through* it.

First Reading   **Jeremiah 1: 4–5, 17–19**

At the outset of what was to prove a very troubled ministry during which his life would more than once be at risk, Jeremiah is assured that God has called him to this particular work and will surely equip him for it. He is not promised easy success; his work will be to wrestle with unbelief, indifference and false confidence. The situation was a critical one for the world of that time. Jeremiah was born about 650 BC. Assyria – a brutal and fierce power – had passed its peak. Marauding bands of Scythians swept down from the north and harassed Palestine. In 612 Assyria collapsed and Babylon came to power. Called to his ministry in 627 BC, it was to a troubled situation, in which powerful political forces and tough individuals waged war, that Jeremiah was to speak.

Responsorial Psalm   **71 (70)**

℟ *My lips will tell of your help.*

1 In you, O Lord, I take refuge;
    let me never be put to shame.
    In your justice rescue me, free me:
    pay heed to me and save me. (R)

2 Be a rock where I can take refuge,
    a mighty stronghold to save me;
    for you are my rock, my stronghold.
    Free me from the hand of the wicked. (R)

3 It is you, O Lord, who are my hope,
  my trust, O Lord, since my youth.
  On you have I leaned from my birth,
  from my mother's womb you have been my help. (R)

4 My lips will tell of your justice
  and day by day of your help.
  O God, you have taught me from my youth
  and I proclaim your wonders still. (R)

A prayer for deliverance from trouble. But it is the confident prayer of him who knows that God sees his plight and will indeed rescue.

Second Reading   **1 Corinthians 12: 31 – 13: 13**

This hymn in praise of love is the pattern of Jesus' own 'excellent way' and is therefore also the ideal set before the Christian. Paul notes the gifts which might seem more eminent (and therefore more to be desired) within the Church – oratorical brilliance, prophetic insight, intellectual acumen, creative faith – and claims that all, without love, are as nothing. He then describes love in all its simple modesty and unselfseeking. Finally he reveals why love is so much more important than every other virtue; it is because love endures. Love belongs to the very being of God (indeed 'God is love', 1 John 4: 8, 16), so that every manifestation of true love is in some sense a disclosure of God. For all its apparent vulnerability and frailty, it is love that remains into all eternity.

Gospel   **Luke 4: 21–30**

The prophet Jeremiah, often rejected, foreshadows the Christ who from the outset met with opposition. As Jesus announced the fulfil-ment of Old Testament promises, men marvelled. But as he ex-plained further, the mood changed. For he showed, citing hints from the Old Testament itself, that God's love for Israel was not exclusive; it was God's intention to work, through his chosen people, for the well-being of all. Religious people seem keen to restrict the divine love to themselves! Yet God's love triumphs – verse 30 hints at the ultimate sovereignty of divine love which human enmity cannot overwhelm.

Fifth Sunday in Ordinary Time

God calls and God equips. God who discloses himself to individual men is never a 'private' God to be kept secretly to oneself; he is the God who in the very act of self-disclosure, commissions a man to tell others also of what he has seen and heard.

First Reading   Isaiah 6: 1–8

The year is 742 BC, the scene is the Jerusalem Temple. Worship is taking place; God's sovereignty is being proclaimed and re-affirmed. As the incense smoke casts a haze of semi-reality over the scene, Isaiah sees, as it were through the mist, the heavenly reality behind it. God is seated in majesty, a God of holiness, glory and power – yet a God who has chosen to commune with a fallen world. Isaiah feels called to take the knowledge of God to his people. Isaiah is intensely aware, in the face of God's holiness, of his own utter unworthiness; he must be pardoned and renewed before he can be of service to God or man.

Responsorial Psalm   138 (137)

℟ *Before the angels I will bless you, O Lord.*

1 I thank you, Lord, with all my heart,
   you have heard the words of my mouth.
   Before the angels I will bless you.
   I will adore before your holy temple. (R)

2 I thank you for your faithfulness and love
   which excel all we ever knew of you.
   On the day I called, you answered;
   you increased the strength of my soul. (R)

3 All earth's kings shall thank you
   when they hear the words of your mouth.
   They shall sing of the Lord's ways:
   'How great is the glory of the Lord!' (R)

4 You stretch out your hand and save me,
   your hand will do all things for me.
   Your love, O Lord, is eternal,
   discard not the work of your hands. (R)

This Psalm is both a thanksgiving and a prayer. God has been gracious; he knows the situation of the psalmist and has delivered him from some plight. Because God has shown himself faithful in this, the psalmist is confident in praying for further, future deliverance.

Second Reading   **1 Corinthians 15: 1–11**

Here is a summary of the gospel message as Paul claims to have received it from others. The 'saving events' can be summed up as the death and resurrection of Jesus. That Jesus died was common knowledge to all living in Palestine at the time. That he was raised to new life, breaking the hold of death, was at first disclosed only to that select number to whom had been given a tangible token of his present, living reality. Paul regarded himself as such a witness, having received (on the Damascus road) a blinding insight into the living reality of Jesus. This vision (like Isaiah's) was not only a conversion experience but a commissioning as well. And as with Isaiah, it brought home to Paul his own utter unworthiness. He was called to knowledge and service by the sheer goodness which lies at the heart of God and of the gospel.

Gospel   **Luke 5: 1–11**

Here is another confrontation and commission. The occasion is early in Jesus' public ministry when the eager crowds pressed on him to hear his words and see his impressive works. For practical reasons Jesus teaches from a boat. Then, maybe to repay Simon's kindness, Jesus puts him in the way of a large catch. We notice Peter's scepticism; it gives way to a kind of reluctant obedience. We notice, too, how in the face of Jesus' power – too much really for comfort – Peter and his companions are not only astonished, but Peter is made acutely aware of his unworthiness and is ashamed. In this disclosure of Jesus' sovereignty comes also Peter's commission – a call to proclaim Jesus to others, which is all-demanding, wholly consuming (cf. v. 11).

Sixth Sunday in Ordinary Time

Only in God, the Father of Jesus Christ, is there the assurance that hope will not be disappointed and trust not prove vain.

First Reading   **Jeremiah 17: 5–8**

The prophet poses a stark contrast. To rely on self, some fellow man, power-politics or military might, is bound to disappoint as surely as a bush in a desert is doomed to wither and die. To trust in the goodness and faithfulness of God is certain to bear fruit, just as will a tree planted in a favoured, well-watered spot. The situation to which Jeremiah addressed his message (about 605 BC) was one of great political instability; Israel's leaders tended to look for military support from within or around the nation. Jeremiah is adamant that the solution to all life's problems (military, political and social ones included) lies in the personal sphere of trust in and loyalty to God.

Responsorial Psalm   1

℟ *Happy the man who has placed*
  his trust in the Lord.

1 Happy indeed is the man
  who follows not the counsel of the wicked;
  nor lingers in the way of sinners
  nor sits in the company of scorners,
  but whose delight is the law of the Lord
  and who ponders his law day and night. (R)

2 He is like a tree that is planted
  beside the flowing waters,
  that yields its fruit in due season
  and whose leaves shall never fade;
  and all that he does shall prosper. (R)

3 Not so are the wicked, not so!
  For they like winnowed chaff
  shall be driven away by the wind.
  For the Lord guards the way of the just
  but the way of the wicked leads to doom. (R)

The psalmist rejoices in his conviction that to trust in God and to walk in his ways must ultimately prove rewarding.

Second Reading   **1 Corinthians 15: 12, 16–20**

Many problems seem to have afflicted the small Christian community at Corinth, problems of faith and of behaviour. In this chapter, Paul responds to the view of some there that Jesus was not raised following his crucifixion (possibly holding that though his body had died, his soul had survived). Paul will have nothing of this. The dichotomy between a perishable body and an immortal soul is probably one with which, anyway, he did not agree. And his conviction is that just as surely as Jesus was put to death on Calvary, so as surely he was raised in his fulness, body and soul. Christianity is not merely the dissemination of ideas but the proclamation of certain events, the history of Jesus. If this history is untrue, then we trust in him in vain. But – such is Paul's conviction – it *is true* (Christ *is* risen) and our hope in him is secure.

Gospel   **Luke 6: 17, 20–26**

Luke's so-called Sermon on the Plain opens (as does Matthew's parallel Sermon on the Mount) with the Beatitudes. Here we have four blessings and four woes. They are to be congratulated whose way of life will be assuredly blessed; they are to be pitied whose stance is such that they are headed for certain downfall. In essence, this message is akin to Jeremiah's and to the psalmist's. Trust God and you will be blessed; trust and serve some false 'god' and you will be let down. What is startlingly new is the recognition that trust in God, far from meaning that immediately all will be well, actually leads to deprivation and loss – and *only so* to fulfilment, affirmation and life.

Seventh Sunday in Ordinary Time

Today's readings concern forgiveness. God is a holy, righteous God in whose sight treachery and apostasy (not to mention our innumerable 'lesser' sins) cannot be a matter of indifference. Yet he is a God who in mercy pardons his wilful and lost creatures.

First Reading   1 Samuel 26: 2, 7–9, 12–13, 22–23

In many respects, Saul had acted towards David with quite irrational and unjustified suspicion and antagonism. He was already showing himself unfitted to continue as Israel's king. In contrast, David comes before us as one well-suited to replace him, and our sympathies may be with Abishai as he argues for taking this seemingly providential opportunity to rid Israel of a second-rate leader. Yet, for all his flaws, Saul remained God's 'anointed' and David cannot bring himself to put down him whom God accepts.

Responsorial Psalm   103 (102)

℟ *The Lord is compassion and love.*

1 My soul, give thanks to the Lord,
   all my being, bless his holy name.
   My soul, give thanks to the Lord
   and never forget all his blessings. (R)

2 It is he who forgives all your guilt,
   who heals every one of your ills,
   who redeems your life from the grave,
   who crowns you with love and compassion. (R)

3 The Lord is compassion and love,
   slow to anger and rich in mercy.
   He does not treat us according to our sins
   nor repay us according to our faults. (R)

4 As far as the east is from the west
   so far does he remove our sins.
   As a father has compassion on his sons,
   the Lord has pity on those who fear him. (R)

In this Psalm the deliverance is not from political threats or the injustices of some enemy; rather, it is deliverance from God's own displeasure. Before God the psalmist is guilty and deserves to die. But God pardons the sinner and redeems the situation, bringing good out of the apparent hopelessness.

Second Reading   **1 Corinthians 15: 45–49**

The psalmist's experience is, according to Paul, the common experience of every man. All are alienated from God because all have sinned. Such is the way we are put together. Adam is made, as the biblical narrative puts it, 'out of dust'; that means that he cannot sustain his own life, he can live only as God breathes into him, only as long as he lives humbly and dependently out of God's hand. But with Jesus the situation is different. Jesus has 'life in himself' (John 5: 26) and is therefore able to bring others to life. Paul affirmed that we share solidarity with frail Adam because that is the way things are; but we also share solidarity with new Adam, the heavenly, living and life-giving Man, because that is the gracious decision of God, who wills us to live in him.

Gospel   **Luke 6: 27–38**

Life 'in Christ' is radically different from 'life in Adam'. The pattern of arrogant, even ruthless, self-assertion which is characteristic of man, gives place to the gentle, undemanding spirit of him who came 'not to be ministered to but to minister and to give his life a ransom for many' (Mark 10: 45). So Jesus' exhortations here to give, to suffer and to serve, are simply encouragements to live as befits those whose life is 'hid with Christ in God' (Colossians 3: 3). This whole new way of life is summarized in verse 36. God is compassionate, not pressing his case against us. If we believe this, then we are challenged to reflect it in our relationships with others.

Eighth Sunday in Ordinary Time

We are forcibly reminded of the enormous gaps that sometimes exist between what is professed with the lips and what is practised in life.

First Reading   **Ecclesiasticus 27: 4–7**

Ecclesiasticus is a work influenced by Greek thinking yet we find the characteristically Hebrew awareness that true wisdom involves not merely thinking right thoughts but behaving as God intends. The author 'teaches that there is only one way whereby a truly wise life can be lived, namely, by living in accordance with the divine commandments; hence his identification of Wisdom with the Law . . .' Our particular verses relate to a man's integrity and inner worth. How should one assess a man? The answer is: a person's true stance in life, his values, his allegiances, his understanding of things, are all disclosed in his speech, because in his talk a man reveals what is truly present in his mind and in his heart.

Responsorial Psalm   92 (91)

℟ *It is good to give you thanks, O Lord.*

1 It is good to give thanks to the Lord
   to make music to your name, O Most High,
   to proclaim your love in the morning
   and your truth in the watches of the night. (R)

2 The just will flourish like the palm-tree
   and grow like a Lebanon cedar. (R)

3 Planted in the house of the Lord
   they will flourish in the courts of our God,
   still bearing fruit when they are old,
   still full of sap, still green,
   to proclaim that the Lord is just.
   In him, my rock, there is no wrong. (R)

God is worthy to be worshipped, because he is faithful to the man who lives uprightly, making him fruitful and prosperous. The psalmist raises for us a question which the Old Testament is aware of but which is not finally answered except in the death and resurrection of Jesus: the problem that the just man, in hard experience, often does *not* seem to be blessed (conversely, the wicked man, in practical terms, often enough flourishes).

Second Reading   1 Corinthians 15: 54–58

In these verses Paul explores something of the relationship between empirical facts and a Christian's inner disposition. Empirically we sin; God's law makes us acutely aware of our sin; death is the result (cf. Genesis 2: 17). These facts stand before us, mocking all human endeavour, all striving, all acquiring (this is the 'sting' of which Paul writes). But the inner conviction of the Christian is that Jesus, by his death, has somehow accomplished a victory over sin and death; his mortality has already achieved immortality. Though such a transformation is not yet ours, it is possible already to share in Christ's victory and so to find the 'sting' of sin and death already drawn.

Gospel   Luke 6: 39–45

Here are two pieces of practical wisdom. The first concerns that strong human tendency to censoriousness. How quickly men judge one another! Jesus did not come amongst us to condemn, not even to condemn those who were obviously 'beyond the pale' (cf. John 3: 17). The Christian is to cultivate similar non-judgemental attitudes. Notice that there is no indifference to the brother's condition; the point is that *in order to be of service to him* our own appalling condition must first be righted.

The second piece of wisdom reminds us of the verses from Ecclesiasticus. If the heart is corrupt, behaviour cannot be good; if the heart is pure, behaviour cannot be rotten. As with much of Jesus' teaching, there is exaggeration here. Reality is not altogether black and white like this and with most of us the heart is partly good and partly bad; consequently our behaviour tends to be the usual mixture. The comment has relevance, however, in understanding how to remedy things; it is not enough to change the outward forms of things; the heart has itself to be changed (cf. Psalm 51: 10).

Ninth Sunday in Ordinary Time

God loves *us*: but does he really love outsiders too? Today's passages remind us that the God of Israel, the God of the Church, is the God also of *all* men.

First Reading   1 Kings 8: 41–43

The occasion of these verses was the dedication of the Temple which David had projected (2 Samuel 7) but which Solomon had built. All the furnishing had been supplied and the Ark of the Covenant had been brought in and placed within the sanctuary. In his dedicatory prayer, Solomon asks that this central shrine might be a place of prayer for Israel, God's special people. Yet he envisages a wider reference: even the visitor from abroad should find in the Temple a haven and a place of meeting with Israel's God. Such a broad perspective is seldom so explicit within the Old Testament, though it *is* present as a small seed and it flowers in the later chapters of Isaiah.

Responsorial Psalm   117 (116)

℟ *Go out to the whole world*
  and proclaim the Good News.
  or *Alleluia!*

1 Alleluia!
  O praise the Lord, all you nations,
  acclaim him all you peoples!
  Strong is his love for us;
  he is faithful for ever. (℟)

The psalmist calls on neighbouring nations to join with him in God's praise; God's faithfulness towards Israel is something which must evoke the adoration of others too. Behind the invitation is clearly the thought that this merciful and faithful God is concerned for the entire world and his goodness towards Israel is token of his goodness towards all. Hence the challenge of the response from Mark's Gospel: if God loves all, then tell all!

Second Reading   Galatians 1: 1–2, 6–10

Paul's mission to the churches of Galatia had brought the knowledge of Jesus and of the redemption achieved through his death and resurrection. Shortly after leaving Galatia, trouble-makers had arrived and had persuaded his converts that in fact Paul was not preaching the true and full gospel (probably these opponents were conservative-Jewish Christians from Jerusalem who were insisting that Gentile converts to Christianity should adhere to Jewish practices such as circumcision and strict dietary laws). Paul replies that there is only one gospel: it is the proclamation that Jesus has disclosed God to man, has represented (in his death and resurrection) man to God, and has reconciled the entire world to God. There *is* no other news that is good and this news is not relative or partial.

Gospel   **Luke 7: 1–10**

Immediately prior to this passage Luke has recorded the 'Sermon on the Plain' (akin to Matthew's 'Sermon on the Mount') which ended with the reminder (Luke 6: 46) that simply mouthing affirmations of loyalty does not constitute discipleship; what matters is making Jesus the basis for living and dying (6: 49). We might well expect at this point that Luke will now illustrate such true faith by showing how God's people did, in fact, put their trust in Jesus. But not so! It is a *Gentile* who expresses complete trust in Jesus' authority to heal (though this centurion is described as 'worthy', it appears that he is no more than a sympathiser; he is not a proselyte to Judaism). Faith, the willingness to take God at his word and to trust him, is not restricted to religious people – which is why the Last Judgement will bring such surprises (cf. Matthew 25: 31–46).

Tenth Sunday in Ordinary Time

Today's readings all concern resurrection. Man lives in a strange tension, longing above all else to live yet having to die. Death casts its shadow over all man's striving and achieving, all his relationships and all his acquisitions. But the biblical witness points towards a life that is not subject to tyrant death but triumphs even over the grave.

First Reading   **1 Kings 17: 17–24**

A widow's son dies tragically and his death is interpreted by his mother as a judgement on her sin. Such is the power of the 'man of God' in the story that he is able to restore the son to life. The conclusion of the narrative is that this capacity confirms the prophet's status as true man of God and confirms his word as genuine word of God (in contrast to the ineffective words of the false prophets). Looking back from the standpoint of the New Testament, we may well want to see in the story a pale anticipation of the yet more glorious resurrection of the Son who was raised by the power of God and reigns at God's right hand.

Responsorial Psalm   **30 (29)**

℟ *I will praise you, Lord, you have rescued me.*

1 I will praise you, Lord, you have rescued me
   and have not let my enemies rejoice over me.
   O Lord, you have raised my soul from the dead,
   restored me to life from those who sink into the grave. (R)

2 Sing psalms to the Lord, you who love him,
   give thanks to his holy name.
   His anger lasts a moment; his favour all through life.
   At night there are tears, but joy comes with dawn. (R)

3 The Lord listened and had pity.
   The Lord came to my help.
   For me you have changed my mourning into dancing;
   O Lord my God, I will thank you for ever. (R)

The psalmist vividly recalls that he had descended already to the place of the dead, but that God in mercy had reached down and snatched him back from the grave. Revived, he invites others to join him in giving thanks to God. Yet he has learned from this bitter experience. He has learned that God hears the cry of those who call upon him. He has learned that easy triumphalism is a fantasy; God's love and goodness are experienced not as we avoid pain and loss, sorrow and sickness, but as we find God *in* these experiences, leading us through them into greater awareness of himself.

Second Reading   **Galatians 1: 11–19**

Paul continues (cf. last week's reading) to oppose the trouble-makers who had so disturbed his converts in Galatia. The gospel of Christ (he argues) is not a philosophical system, constructed by man's wisdom – for Paul did not receive it from men, not even from the 'pillar' apostles in Jerusalem. The gospel which had so transformed Paul's behaviour had burst into his life in the dramatic self-disclosure of Jesus on the Damascus road. The truth of the gospel is not authenticated by certain authorized people; it authenticates itself as Jesus makes himself real 'from faith to faith' (Romans 1: 17) and as men reach out to him in trust and hope.

Gospel   **Luke 7: 11–17**

The twin themes that we encountered in the Elijah story reappear here. Jesus raises the dead son to life, indicating his power even over the grave. And the people marvel, acknowledging that this display of power authenticates Jesus as indeed a man of God. The breaking in of life into the sphere of death indicates the presence of God in the affairs of men (so v. 16). Of course, the story is a parable (though also a real event); the dead son lived on for who knows how many years, only later to die again. But he points to the one who 'has life in himself' (John 5: 26) and who, entering the realm of decay and death, emptied it of its sting and its hold on man.

Eleventh Sunday in Ordinary Time

Today's theme, central to the Christian understanding of things, is repentance and forgiveness. Whatever modern man has discovered about the degree to which (through genetic heritage or through environment) we all are 'programmed' to be the kind of people we are, human experience knows that we nevertheless have some room to 'be ourselves'; and, strangely, 'being ourselves' involves a rebelliousness that is in our own worst interests, it involves us in sin which destroys. How to find pardon and peace in this freely-chosen waywardness is man's deepest need.

First Reading   **2 Samuel 12: 7–10, 13**

Like so many failures, David's sin began with lust; he wanted what it was not legitimate, nor indeed possible, for him to possess. The story is told in chapter eleven and it is a sad and sordid tale of intrigue and treachery, the result of which is the arranged death of Uriah and the marriage of David to Bathsheba. All appears to have gone well, but 'the thing that David had done displeased the Lord'! Nathan is sent off to bring home to the king the shameful nature of his act and he does this through the moving story of the rich man who slaughters his poor neighbour's only lamb to feed a passing guest. David had the wit to see the dastardly nature of his sin and to repent. In response, he is assured that his sin is pardoned, though its consequences remain real.

Responsorial Psalm   32 (31)

℟ *Forgive, Lord, the guilt of my sin.*

1 Happy the man whose offence is forgiven,
    whose sin is remitted.
    O happy the man to whom the Lord
    imputes no guilt,
    in whose spirit is no guile. (R)

2 But now I have acknowledged my sins;
    my guilt I did not hide.
    I said: 'I will confess
    my offence to the Lord.'
    And you, Lord, have forgiven
    the guilt of my sin. (R)

3 You are my hiding place, O Lord;
    you save me from distress.
    You surround me with cries of deliverance. (R)

4 Rejoice, rejoice in the Lord,
    exult, you just!
    O come, ring out your joy,
    all you upright of heart. (R)

God can be relied on to pardon; it belongs to his nature to care for recalcitrant man and rescue him even in his rebellion and wandering. This pardon meets a man at the point of his repentance; God does not pardon a man *because* he repents (as though man took the initiative and God acted in response) – yet without penitence, God's pardon finds no lodging in a man.

Second Reading   **Galatians 2: 16, 19–21**

Paul continues his argument against the trouble-makers in Galatia. Being made right with God happens (he maintains) not by *our* doing or saying what is required, nor by *our* being in a favourable position; there is nothing from the side of man which would encourage God to act graciously towards him (v. 16). Rather it all stems from God, who in the death of Jesus has taken up the whole created order and judged it – and in the resurrection of Jesus has made it all anew. This (spelled out in greater length in, e.g., Colossians 1) is the basis on which Paul can so boldly affirm 'I have been crucified with Christ . . .' (v. 20).

Gospel   Luke 7: 36–8: 3

The religious man ('the Pharisee') easily forgets that he is as un-acceptable to God as any rank outsider; that before God we are all empty-handed, all beggars. The man who knows this is like the character in the parable, who was forgiven a massive debt and who, as a consequence, was immensely grateful. The other character in the story was also a debtor, but being less conscious of this he was also less conscious of the marvel of forgiveness. 'It should be noted that Simon had not acted discourteously; he had been correct enough as a host, but had not performed any special acts of hospitality that went beyond the mere demands of the situation' (I. H. Marshall). But the provision by the woman of water, a kiss and oil, lavishing upon Jesus almost exaggerated devotion, expressed her gratitude for pardon much needed and gladly received.

Twelfth Sunday in Ordinary Time

In his letter to the Philippians (3: 20) Paul says that our citizenship is in heaven, from which we await a Saviour; we are only passing pilgrims on earth, no matter how significant life is here and now. Our stance as Christians must always include a certain restless longing for what awaits us.

First Reading   Zechariah 12: 10–11

The theme is sorrow; a God-given spirit of compassion which leads the inhabitants of Jerusalem to weep as one mourns over a lost child, a broken relationship, a sin committed. It is impossible to tell to what particular situation (if any) the prophet refers – it may be that he is thinking in generalities and of life as a whole. It is also far from clear what is meant by 'him whom they have pierced' (some manuscripts have '*me* whom they have pierced'); it may be we should look for an historical character (Onias, high priest murdered in the second century BC would be an obvious candidate); it may be that we have a reference here to that enigmatic figure, the Suffering Servant of Isaiah; or (if we take the reading 'me') it might be a reference to sighing after God whom we have offended ('pierced' understood now metaphorically) but who graciously draws near to us in our need.

Responsorial Psalm   **63 (62)**

℟ *For you my soul is thirsting,*
  O God, my God.

1 O God, you are my God, for you I long;
  for you my soul is thirsting.
  My body pines for you
  like a dry, weary land without water. (R)

2 So I gaze on you in the sanctuary
  to see your strength and your glory.
  For your love is better than life,
  my lips will speak your praise. (R)

3 So I will bless you all my life,
  in your name I will lift up my hands.
  My soul shall be filled as with a banquet,
  my mouth shall praise you with joy. (R)

4 For you have been my help;
  in the shadow of your wings I rejoice.
  My soul clings to you;
  your right hand holds me fast. (R)

There is here a wistful longing which is characteristic of men not only in moments of acute need, but even in moments of blessing. Experiences of good can stir such longings for fulfilment and satisfaction.

Second Reading   **Galatians 3: 26–29**

Longing and waiting: here is the theme again, for it is clear that what
Paul affirms to be true 'in Christ' is not yet true in our empirical
day-to-day lives. One family we may indeed be, but church divisions
are real and seemingly intractable. Maybe we are neither slave nor
free, but in practice some are certainly more free than others. So Paul
turns without hesitation to the thought of the 'heir' (see 4: 1–7); as
heirs of the promises to Abraham and to the people of the old
covenant we inherit what they only looked forward to. But as 'heirs'
we ourselves also strain forward to that which is still outstanding, the
full experience of our inheritance.

Gospel   **Luke 9: 18–24**

Here is the heart of the Christian's unease; he not only longs for the
full inheritance of which he is heir, but he treads meanwhile a path
which is full of distress and pain, a path which is soberingly like that
which led Christ himself to Calvary. For if we are to inherit that
which Jesus has already procured for us, it is necessary that we
should walk his way, the way of self-forgetfulness and self-loss (v.
22). Mankind seeks to live by arrogant self-assertiveness, but he
finds, in fact, only the grave ('whoever would save his life will lose
it'). The new man, the second Adam, treads the way that accepts
loss, he allows himself to be negated – and he finds thereby life
('whoever loses his life . . . will save it'). And the life that is found
through this acceptance of loss is life which not even the grave can
suppress.

Thirteenth Sunday in Ordinary Time

A leading theme in today's readings is the cost of discipleship.

First Reading   **1 Kings 19: 16, 19–21**

Elijah is pictured as the one who anoints kings and prophets. The
anointing of a prophet is unusual in the Old Testament but here it
probably signifies that the prophet's status is no less than that of the

king. Elijah will be an agent of God in the shaping of history. The prophet casts his mantle over Elisha to indicate his claim over him as a disciple. Elijah's reply to Elisha's request (v. 20) appears to be a rebuke: 'Go! Return! For what have *I* (unlike your mother and father) done for you?' When a disciple/prophet is called he cannot look back. In the event Elisha does not go back but instead destroys his old means of livelihood as a demonstration of his commitment to Elijah. By the feast he also shows that his concern is not now for his family but for the people as a whole.

Responsorial Psalm   16 (15)

℟ *O Lord, it is you who are my portion.*

1 Preserve me, God, I take refuge in you.
  I say to the Lord: 'You are my God.'
  O Lord, it is you who are my portion and cup;
  it is you yourself who are my prize. (R)

2 I will bless the Lord who gives me counsel,
  who even at night directs my heart.
  I keep the Lord ever in my sight:
  since he is at my right hand, I shall stand firm. (R)

3 And so my heart rejoices, my soul is glad;
  even my body shall rest in safety.
  For you will not leave my soul among the dead,
  nor let your beloved know decay. (R)

4 You will show me the path of life,
  the fullness of joy in your presence,
  at your right hand happiness for ever. (R)

A psalm of confidence or trust. God himself is the disciple's inheritance. God shows us the path of life.

Second Reading   **Galatians 5: 1, 13–18**

The freedom Paul is speaking of is freedom, in faith, from the confines of the 'law' ('a yoke of slavery'). But he realizes that freedom from the law might be taken to mean a licence for immorality. Thus he looks for a moral principle to use in his teaching and finds it in the concept of 'love'. Indeed he observes that the commandment to love one's neighbour as oneself (Leviticus 19: 18; cf. Jesus' use of the text in Mark 12: 31) undergirds the whole of the Jewish law. While 'neighbour' in Leviticus probably means 'fellow-Israelite', here it is clear that Paul puts no such limitations on its meaning. A Church that is divided by factions is not a loving church but a self-destroying one.

Verses 16 and 17 explore further the contrast of 'flesh' and 'spirit'. While Paul does not see 'flesh' as inherently evil, he recognizes that it is in the sphere of man's ordinary corporal existence that sin makes its inroads. Accordingly people must 'walk by the spirit'. The term 'spirit' may have its general sense of the spiritual life (you must cultivate your spiritual life) or it may refer to the Spirit of God (you must let your life be controlled by God's Spirit). The phrase, 'to prevent you from doing what you would' (v. 17) is difficult. The Greek word introducing it usually implies purpose: the opposition of spirit and flesh is designed to prevent you doing what you wish. But it may here express result: this opposition results in a loss of freedom of action.

Gospel   **Luke 9: 51–62**

The reading focuses on the nature of Jesus' own mission and the cost of discipleship. The Samaritans (descendants of Israelites and foreigners from an earlier period) had long been at odds with the Jews. The fact that Jesus intended to go to the Jewish centre at Jerusalem was enough to lead them to reject him. It is not they, however, who are rebuked, but James and John (the sons of thunder!) who mistakenly see Jesus' role as that of an Elijah, in confrontation with kings and calling down fire from heaven (2 Kings 1). The meaning of discipleship is illustrated in three meetings. The first man asks to be allowed to follow Jesus. Jesus points to the total commitment necessary – the Son of Man has not even the comforts of the wild animals. The second man is called to follow but asks first to be allowed to bury his father. For a Jew this burial would have been a wholly necessary duty as well as an act of love. By his seeming harshness Jesus makes crystal clear where the priorities lie – discipleship comes before either personal feeling or traditional duties. (The 'dead' are those who are not alive to the message of the kingdom.) The third man who wishes to follow, like Elisha responding to Elijah's call, wishes first to take leave of his parents. Again the urgency of discipleship is made plain to him.

Fourteenth Sunday in Ordinary Time

God's action, past, present and future, is one thing we can with certainty rejoice in, indeed boast in.

First Reading   **Isaiah 66: 10–14**

The prophet, probably not Isaiah of Jerusalem but an anonymous figure of the exilic (sixth century BC) or early post-exilic period, sees a vision of a new Jerusalem. A subject of mourning in the prophet's own time (because destroyed, or perhaps a poor, struggling re-settlement after having been long in ruins), the city is pictured as becoming a subject of joy, a mother who will nourish her children ('from the abundance of her glory' in v. 11 may possibly be translated 'from her bountiful breast'). The focus moves to those who will be suckled ('you' – the present inhabitants?) who are identified in verse 14 as the Lord's servants.

Responsorial Psalm   **66 (65)**

℟ *Cry out with joy to God all the earth.*

1 Cry out with joy to God all the earth,
   O sing to the glory of his name.
   O render him glorious praise.
   Say to God: 'How tremendous your deeds!' (R)

2 'Before you all the earth shall bow;
   shall sing to you, sing to your name!'
   Come and see the works of God,
   tremendous his deeds among men. (R)

3 He turned the sea into dry land,
   they passed through the river dry-shod.
   Let our joy then be in him;
   he rules for ever by his might. (R)

4 Come and hear, all who fear God.
  I will tell what he did for my soul.
  Blessed be God who did not reject my prayer
  nor withhold his love from me. (R)

The psalmist rejoices in what God has done for his nation (at the Exodus) and for him personally. The Psalm is a hymn of thanksgiving (cf. p. 12).

Second Reading   **Galatians 6:14–18**

Paul brings to a conclusion his exhortation to the Christians in Galatia against allowing themselves to elevate the requirements of the Jewish Law (especially the practice of circumcision) into a prerequisite of faith. The only thing he can boast about is the cross of Christ. Through Jesus' death and resurrection Paul's own relationship to the world has been transformed. To speak of the world as 'crucified' is probably a vivid way of saying that the demands of his previous life (the unconverted world) no longer have control over him. The issue of circumcision is irrelevant compared to the fact that Christ's coming has meant a transformed world; in effect it is as though the world has been created anew for Paul and all who believe in Christ. The only 'rule' (a reference to the Law) is that of Christ's cross, and those who live by faith in the risen Christ shall make up the true Israel, the Israel of God. The 'marks' of verse 17 may be an allusion to scars left on Paul's body after persecution. As such they would be like the brand-marks of ownership. The letter closes with the word 'brethren' added to the blessing, a touch perhaps of reconciling warmth.

Gospel   **Luke 10: 1–12, 17–20**

In this passage we catch a glimpse of the new kingdom of God breaking in on the old world. The mission of the seventy (cf. the seventy elders chosen by Moses, Exodus 24: 1) parallels that of the twelve (Luke 9) and perhaps foreshadows the universal mission of the disciples after the resurrection. The depicting of the mission as a harvest conveys the sense that the time is ripe for action and decision. The urgency is perhaps reflected in verse 4 in the instruction to travel light and to pause for nothing on the way, not even a polite 'hello'. The missioners have a two-fold role. Their mere appearance in a village, no more, is significant in itself. It is up to the villagers to recognize them for what they are, namely heralds of the kingdom. In the very act of receiving or not receiving these strangers the villagers make a choice for or against the kingdom (cf. Matthew 25: 35–40). Where the missioners are received they have a second task: they must heal the sick (cf. 'the demons are subject to us in your name', v. 17) and announce quite specifically the nearness of the kingdom (near not just in time, but in place – it is a present reality which has come close). Where there is rejection there is to be no delay, simply the announcement. Verse 12 makes clear that acceptance or rejection of the kingdom is a matter of life and death (for Sodom's destruction see Genesis 19: 24, 28). The joy of the seventy (who address Jesus by his messianic title, 'Lord') is capped by Jesus' summing up (v. 18): the fall of Satan, the overpowering of death, is what the kingdom is all about. The last verse adds a note of warning. It is dangerous to rejoice in your own newly won power; let it be sufficient to know that you are a member of the kingdom.

Fifteenth Sunday in Ordinary Time

May the meaning of Christianity be summed up in the 'golden rule'?

First Reading   **Deuteronomy 30: 10–14**

The passage comes from Moses' address to the people following the giving of the great code of law on Mount Sinai. The people are still in the no-man's land beyond their old home in Egypt and far from the one promised them. This part of the book of Deuteronomy has probably been moulded to its present shape in the period of exile in Babylon in the sixth century BC (cf. Isaiah 40–55) when Israel faced the same choice as in the days of Moses – the choice whether or not to accept a partnership (covenant) with God, abiding by his moral and religious law, and risk the journey (return) with him to the promised land. Verses 12 and 13 present, in a pictorial way, the point that the passage stresses: God's law is clear for every ordinary person to see and to understand. It doesn't require great effort (of mind or body) to be grasped. It is obvious and easy to obey. We are reminded, perhaps, of Jesus' designation of the kingdom of God as near at hand for those who choose to see it.

Responsorial Psalm   **69 (68)**

℟ *Seek the Lord, you who are poor,*
  and your hearts will revive.

1 This is my prayer to you,
  my prayer for your favour.
  In your great love, answer me, O God,
  with your help that never fails:
  Lord, answer, for your love is kind;
  in your compassion, turn towards me. (R)

2 As for me in my poverty and pain
  let your help, O God, lift me up.
  I will praise God's name with a song;
  I will glorify him with thanksgiving. (R)

3 The poor when they see it will be glad
  and God-seeking hearts will revive;
  for the Lord listens to the needy
  and does not spurn his servants in their chains. (R)

4 For God will bring help to Zion
  and rebuild the cities of Judah.
  The sons of his servants shall inherit it;
  those who love his name shall dwell there. (R)

The Psalm is a lament of the individual (cf. p. 12). The psalmist has suffered from some illness; his family are not sympathetic and his enemies have taken the opportunity to make unjust accusations against him.

Second Reading   **Colossians 1: 15–20**

This is one of Paul's most striking accounts of the nature of Jesus' divinity. Many of the terms used in the description remind us of the role of the 'Wisdom' of God in the Old Testament (Job 28, Psalm 33, Proverbs 8, Ecclesiasticus 24, Wisdom 7). Through God's wisdom the world was created, and by it he rules all things and all things make sense, cohere, because of it. But Wisdom was also closely connected with the Law (Torah) in Jewish thought of the time. Accordingly there is the suggestion in the Christian hymn that Christ is not only the embodiment of God's wisdom, he is also the new Law. There are many difficulties in this passage, but the heart of it is Paul's conviction of the centrality of Christ's death and resurrection in revealing his true significance. He is 'first-born from the dead' and his great role of peace-making ('reconciling all things' – restoring harmony to everything) comes through 'the blood of his cross'.

Gospel   **Luke 10: 25–37**

Jesus here teaches a lawyer (probably a theologian) the meaning of the Law. The heart of it is already evident in Old Testament passages well recognized by the Jewish theologians ('You shall love the Lord your God' etc., Deuteronomy 6: 5, Leviticus 19: 18). But what the story of the Samaritan shows is that in practice the *legalism* that had pervaded Jewish religion had obscured this heart. Jew and Samaritan were at loggerheads on issues of religious orthodoxy, arguing about whose rules and worship were authentic. Yet the priest and Levite (a kind of priest), pillars of Judaism, could so forget what their religion really meant as to pass by the injured man, no doubt for fear of becoming involved in any ensuing obligations if the man should die (contact with a corpse would make them 'impure' and so unable to take part in worship). But the Law is fulfilled in the showing of mercy (cf. Micah 6: 8); and in the parable it is fulfilled by the despised heretic, the Samaritan. Jesus seems to be saying that the true fulfilment of the Law is within reach of all, but is being denied by a preoccupation with its outward rather than its inward nature.

Sixteenth Sunday in Ordinary Time

It is all too easy to assume that we know what tasks God might expect us to undertake and what roles in life he judges to be most worthwhile – but we might all too easily be mistaken.

First Reading   **Genesis 18: 1–10**

Abraham is an old man and his wife Sarah has been unable to bear
children. At his wife's suggestion Abraham has had a son, Ishmael,
by Sarah's maid, Hagar, but this has brought not happiness but
division within the family (Genesis 16). Then God promises Abraham that Sarah will indeed bear a son: 'I will bless her and she shall
be a mother of nations' (Genesis 17: 16). Abraham can only laugh.
Now he is again visited by the Lord in the company of two others,
though Abraham seems to see merely three travellers to whom he
offers warm hospitality. This is in fact the visit of God and it marks
the bestowal of blessing, the conception of the child. The story goes
on to say that at the suggestion that she should bear a child Sarah
herself laughs. The outcome of the story (Genesis 21) is the birth of
Isaac (his name is a pun on the Hebrew word 'to laugh'). The laugh is
on Abraham and Sarah. God's promise of the child is fulfilled and the
promise of a nation is brought a step closer.

Responsorial Psalm   15 (14)

℟ *Lord, who shall be admitted to your tent?*

1 Lord, who shall dwell on your holy mountain?
   He who walks without fault;
   he who acts with justice
   and speaks the truth from his heart;
   he who does not slander with his tongue. (R)

2 He who does no wrong to his brother,
   who casts no slur on his neighbour,
   who holds the godless in disdain,
   but honours those who fear the Lord. (R)

3 He who takes no interest on a loan
   and accepts no bribes against the innocent.
   Such a man will stand firm for ever. (R)

'Who is a fit person to visit God's sanctuary?' asks the psalmist. The
Psalm was perhaps originally used in the liturgy of the Temple: to
the worshipper who asked at the entrance for the conditions of entry,
the answer would be given.

Second Reading **Colossians 1: 24–28**

Paul speaks of the task allotted to him. What is meant by 'completing what is lacking in Christ's afflictions' (v. 24)? Two main suggestions are (*a*) that as a Christian, Paul must share in Christ's sufferings, but yet since he has not yet undergone suffering leading to death he has not completed his experience of 'Christ's afflictions'; (*b*) that there is a certain total or quota of sufferings which the Church, the 'body of Christ', must undergo before it reaches the End (the second coming?), and that by suffering much Paul makes his contribution to the speedy arrival of this longed-for time. The 'mystery' (v. 26) is God's secret purpose as divulged to his people. It is still a mystery in that it is divulged to all, yet few prove capable of seeing and receiving it. It is even more a mystery in that it consists of finding the (Jewish) messiah (Christ) among non-Jews (Gentiles) – 'in among you'. 'Teaching every man in all wisdom' (v. 28) implies that Paul holds nothing back. The gospel is open to all, and Paul is its presenter.

Gospel **Luke 10: 38–42**

This passage has sometimes been used to claim the superiority of the life of meditation and contemplation over the active life; some commentators have seen in it an illustration of the relative priority of the ministry of 'liturgy' over that of the 'diaconate', a warning against a kind of religious business (being busy) that distracts from true concentration upon the essentials of faith. Mary's behaviour may seem unfair but to Jesus the crucial thing is the importance of God's work (Jesus' teaching). Martha, like Abraham in Genesis 18, is concerned to offer the best hospitality. But perhaps then she has missed the point of Jesus' visit.

Seventeenth Sunday in Ordinary Time

Do we really know how, and for what, to pray?

First Reading **Genesis 18: 20–32**

The passage immediately follows the story of Abraham's three guests. Now their identity is revealed – it is God and his messengers

123

(angels). The Lord has received great complaints ('outcry' is the cry for help from someone who is oppressed or abused) against Sodom and Gomorrah. Since he represents justice he is bound to respond in some way. The remarkable scene between God and Abraham explores a serious problem facing the religious believer. Sodom represents a sinful community, *any* community. What should God do? Destroy the community and with it the few who are righteous, or allow a wicked community to continue for the sake of an innocent few? The anxiety of Abraham as he reduces the number who might count as a minimum, reflects his growing astonishment at the growing gap between what might have been expected of human justice and what is revealed of God's justice. The number stops at ten, but the implication is that it would progress to one. The message can be found again in Hosea 11: 8–9.

Responsorial Psalm   **138 (137)**

℟ *On the day I called,*
  you answered me, O Lord.

1 I thank you, Lord, with all my heart,
  you have heard the words of my mouth.
  Before the angels I will bless you.
  I will adore before your holy temple. (R)

2 I thank you for your faithfulness and love
  which excel all we ever knew of you.
  On the day I called, you answered;
  you increased the strength of my soul. (R)

3 The Lord is high yet he looks on the lowly
  and the haughty he knows from afar.
  Though I walk in the midst of affliction
  you give me life and frustrate my foes. (R)

4 You stretch out your hand and save me,
  your hand will do all things for me.
  Your love, O Lord, is eternal,
  discard not the work of your hands. (R)

The Psalm is a thanksgiving either of an individual or of the community (cf. p. 12) which is offering thanks for deliverance from the Babylonian exile.

Second Reading   **Colossians 2: 12–14**

Two main themes emerge: (*a*) God's forgiveness of our sins is seen above all in the events of the cross, the meaning of which is expressed, for example, in baptism; (*b*) Since we are thus set free, there is no reason to allow ourselves to be controlled by all kinds of secondary rules and beliefs. Paul has been looking at the question of what ritual signs and ceremonies are necessary for a person to enter the community of Christ. It would seem that some persons had appeared offering a teaching about secrets that were essential to salvation – information about the 'true' nature of the world, 'the elements of the universe' (v. 20), angelic powers, and what had to be done in order to be in proper accord with them. Paul responds by pointing to baptism. It symbolizes the believer's death to the old life and acceptance of the new (v. 12). Just as God brought Christ to new life, so the believer who was caught in a death-like existence of failure to live up to the ideal ('dead in trespasses') is made truly alive. The rule-bound religion of Israel ('the bond . . . with its legal demands', v. 14) is cancelled, and all demonic 'powers' thought to inhabit the universe made powerless. It is not adherence to rules, mere shadows, but total commitment to Christ, who is real substance, that finally counts (vv. 16–23).

Gospel   **Luke 11: 1–13**

The nature of prayer is explored by practical example (the Lord's prayer) and explanation (the parable of the friend at midnight). The prayer reflects the disciples' situation – standing on the brink of a new age, looking to the arrival of the kingdom of God. As Jesus makes clear in verse 9, the kingdom is a matter of asking and seeking; and there will be no disappointment. A man who will not get up and disturb his whole family even for a friend, will probably do so if the knocking is persistent. How much more likely, then, is God, who is 'father', to respond to the persistent knocking of his children? If sinful man knows how to give appropriate gifts to his children, how much more likely is God to give *his* children the prize gift of all, that of his Spirit?

The prayer: 'daily' seems to mean 'day by day', but the phrase may possibly be taken as 'bread for the *coming* day', perhaps a reference to the imminent arrival of the Kingdom.

Eighteenth Sunday in Ordinary Time

Today's theme is twofold: a warning against false and merely earthly values, and an exhortation to adopt the true values founded on the teaching of Christ.

First Reading   Ecclesiastes 1: 2; 2: 21–23

The book from which this passage is taken was written about the third century BC, by an anonymous writer sometimes referred to as 'the Preacher'. Though not on the highest level of Old Testament revelation, the author's attitude is dominated by sincerity and unshakable faith. His rather pessimistic outlook is influenced by the transitoriness of human life. 'Vanity' translates a Hebrew word whose root meaning is 'breath' or 'vapour', and the author uses it to signify something aimless and passing. 'Vanity of vanities' expresses complete and utter vanity. He sees the work of man as leading apparently nowhere. Indeed his toil seems only to heighten anxiety and the sense of frustration.

Responsorial Psalm   95 (94)

℟ *O that today you would listen to his voice!*
   Harden not your hearts.

1 Come, ring out our joy to the Lord;
   hail the rock who saves us.
   Let us come before him, giving thanks,
   with songs let us hail the Lord. (R)

2 Come in; let us bow and bend low;
   let us kneel before the God who made us
   for he is our God and we
   the people who belong to his pasture,
   the flock that is led by his hand. (R)

3 O that today you would listen to his voice!
   'Harden not your hearts as at Meribah,

as on that day at Massah in the desert
when your fathers put me to the test;
when they tried me, though they saw my work.' (R)

This Psalm begins as a hymn (cf. p. 12) whose sentiments are in
direct contrast to those in the preceding reading. God is no 'vapour',
something transitory, but rather a 'rock', that is solid, permanent
and secure. Accordingly the people should heed the prophetic oracle
that comes from the voice of God, for 'today' is the day of opportunity and decision.

Second Reading   **Colossians 3: 1–5, 9–11**

This passage is part of a larger section concerned with false asceticism. Paul draws a contrast between the 'things that are above' and
the 'things that are on earth'. The Christian must concentrate on
matters of ultimate concern and not on merely earthly trivialities.
Paul is attacking a material type of superstitious ritualism described
earlier in the section. The final verses concern practical implications
of faith. Baptismal symbolism is found in the command to 'put to
death' the former personality; also in the 'stripping off of the old
man' and the 'putting on' of the new man. The theme 'old man' and
'new man' refers primarily to the individual, though it does carry
corporate associations in so much as it forms part of Paul's presenta-
tion of the gospel in terms of the 'earthly man' (Adam) and the
'heavenly man' (Christ). As sinners we are part of the earthly man,
but baptism incorporates us into Christ, the heavenly man.

Gospel   **Luke 12: 13–21**

It was usual for a plaintiff to bring his case to a religious leader since
the Mosaic Law embraced without any distinction criminal, civil,
religious and moral law. The Rabbi (i.e. teacher) was expected to be
proficient in all departments. The title 'Teacher' indicates the standing Jesus had won with the people. Throughout his public life, Jesus
was constantly correcting the confusion that occurred between true
morality and legal systems. In this case he refuses to arbitrate.
Legislation belongs to Caesar; Jesus is concerned with the higher
standards of the Kingdom of God. The law may restrain sinners and

make them law-abiding but it cannot make them good. Only by entering the Kingdom of heaven and living by its moral standards and spiritual resources will a person become good. Then legislation will cease to be relevant. He goes on to show by a parable that abundant life is not to be found in material possessions. The rich fool found this out too late. Material wealth is not a permanent possession. Indeed death disclosed the rich fool's essential poverty. Therefore, the only possessions worth striving for are those which death cannot take away. Therefore Jesus counsels: 'lay up your treasure in heaven'.

Nineteenth Sunday in Ordinary Time

God has chosen us and made us his own. Nevertheless we must be ever watchful so that we shall be found ready when he calls us to our inheritance.

First Reading   **Wisdom 18: 6–9**

The book of Wisdom was written about a century before the birth of Christ. It was attributed to Solomon because of Solomon's reputation for wisdom (see 1 Kings 4: 29–34). In this passage the author is meditating on the night of the Exodus (see Exodus 12: 21–42). On this night the avenging angel 'passed over' the houses of the Israelites but struck down the first-born of the Egyptians. On this night, too, the Israelites escaped from Egyptian captivity and set out for the Promised Land. This saving act of God is what is commemorated each year when Passover is celebrated. The author expands the first passover story with some of the developed Passover ritual of his own time. He brings out three things: that the deliverance from Egypt was part of God's divine plan; that the single act of God both struck down their enemies and raised up the Israelites to freedom; that it was the first passover when they 'offered sacrifice in secret' (as opposed to the later practice of open and public sacrifice).

Responsorial Psalm   **33 (32)**

℟ *Happy are the people the Lord has chosen as his own.*

1 Ring out your joy to the Lord, O you just;
   for praise is fitting for loyal hearts.

They are happy, whose God is the Lord,
the people he has chosen as his own. (R)

2 The Lord looks on those who revere him,
on those who hope in his love,
to rescue their souls from death,
to keep them alive in famine. (R)

3 Our soul is waiting for the Lord.
The Lord is our help and our shield.
May your love be upon us, O Lord,
as we place all our hope in you. (R)

This Psalm is a good example of an Israelite hymn. It begins with a summons to praise God and continues by giving motives for such praise. The conclusion passes on to a prayer that the grace of this moment may govern the life that follows. It aptly gives poetic response to the saving act recounted in the first reading.

Second Reading   **Hebrews 11: 1–2, 8–19**

Chapter eleven of Hebrews speaks about faith. Examples of steadfast and enduring faith are given from the traditions of the Old Testament patriarchs. In the present passage the examples cited as models of faith are Abraham and Sarah. Abraham left his home for an unknown destination because he trusted in God's promise. Sarah believed in the promise made to her that she would have a child. Abraham's faith in God was so unshakable that subsequently he was prepared, at God's command, to sacrifice that very child because he still believed that somehow God's promise that he would be father of a great nation would be fulfilled. The definition of faith in the chapter is a description based on metaphor; it concerns the assurance which suffering and persecuted Christians have that faith is a guarantee of the unseen realities in which they place their hope, namely, the heavenly home towards which they are striving.

Gospel   **Luke 12: 32–48**

The beginning of this reading concerns true and false security. In context it comes at the end of a section in which Jesus has spoken about the contrast between earthly and heavenly possessions (see last

Sunday's Gospel). Now he turns to encouragement, since what he is proposing to them must seem daunting and difficult to attain. Jesus wants them to realize that the Kingdom of heaven is not an other-worldly dream, but a present possession, realized not by their own achievement, but because the Father gives it to them freely.

The passage continues with warnings about the imminent coming of the Son of Man. They must be continually alert. He illustrates the warning with two parables: one about loyal servants who must make sure that at the decisive moment of their master's return they are not caught unawares; the second about a householder who would have taken steps to prevent the thief had he known when he would break into the house. The parable with which Jesus replies to Peter's question has been re-applied and no longer refers to Israel's leaders. The early Christians interpreted it as a warning to the Church's leaders, which is a perfectly natural extension of its meaning.

Twentieth Sunday in Ordinary Time

The Way of the Lord demands a radical choice; hence the message of the prophets and above all the teaching of Christ can cause dissension.

First Reading **Jeremiah 38: 4–6, 8–10**

Jeremiah's plight was the result of King Zedekiah consulting him during the Babylonian siege of Jerusalem in 588 BC. Jeremiah's message was, as always, that events were merely divine judgement which the people brought upon themselves because of their infidelity to the Covenant. The Babylonians were God's instrument of judgement and so the city should surrender and not continue to thwart the will of God. But this message was seen as treason and the death penalty was passed. By casting Jeremiah into the pit they tried to put him to death without bloodshed. However, Jeremiah is rescued through the intervention of an Ethiopian eunuch. This could be seen as another example of God's plans being achieved through human instrumentality (see Jeremiah 1: 8).

Responsorial Psalm   **40 (39)**

℞ *Lord, come to my aid*

1 I waited, I waited for the Lord
   and he stooped down to me;
   he heard my cry. (R)

2 He drew me from the deadly pit,
   from the miry clay.
   He set my feet upon a rock
   and made my footsteps firm. (R)

3 He put a new song into my mouth,
   praise of our God.
   Many shall see and fear
   and shall trust in the Lord. (R)

4 As for me, wretched and poor,
   the Lord thinks of me.
   You are my rescuer, my help,
   O God, do not delay. (R)

This thanksgiving Psalm (cf. p. 12) is chosen here because of its reference to the 'pit' in the second stanza. The 'pit' is a symbol for death, and it is in response to the psalmist's faith that God delivers him. The 'new song' is the present Psalm of thanksgiving inspired by God's saving act.

Second reading   **Hebrews 12: 1–4**

After a survey of Old Testament figures who persevered in faith (see last week's passage), the author returns to the present and exhorts his readers to hold firm in their own faith no matter what the cost. The Christian existence is likened to a school of endurance in which the formation and training are divine. Suffering and vindication are put at the heart of the Christian message, with the death and resurrection of Jesus as the central events of salvation. The lesson, directed towards those who appear to be faltering in faith, is to take Jesus as their model: 'Let us not lose sight of Jesus, who leads us in our faith and brings it to perfection'.

Gospel   **Luke 12: 49–53**

Here Jesus uses imagery that has a long history. In the Old Testament we read of men passing through the fire of testing or overwhelmed by a sea of troubles (see Isaiah 43: 2; Psalm 66: 12; 69: 1–2. Baptism, however, is not an Old Testament word. Here and elsewhere (see Mark 10: 38) Jesus uses it to describe his own death. He is also echoing the teaching of John the Baptist who prophesied the coming of one who would baptize with the fire of divine judgement. Here we are given a glimpse into the mind of Jesus: a mixture of impatience and reluctance to get on with the redemptive plan of God. By his death his mission will be accomplished, but it will also entail his rejection by Israel's leaders. This, inevitably, will bring about the conflict of loyalties that he speaks about in his prophecy of divisions.

Twenty-first Sunday in Ordinary Time

The theme running through today's readings is that salvation is for all.

First Reading   **Isaiah 66: 18–21**

The last chapters (56–66) of Isaiah date from the period after the Exile. They speak about salvation and judgement. In the present passage God's gathering, which elsewhere refers exclusively to the dispersed of Israel, is extended to include all nations and tongues. This phrase makes God's salvation truly universal. The 'sign' could be a signpost pointing out the way, or it could mean the sending of messengers themselves (cf. Isaiah 45: 20–25). The 'survivors of the nations' are invited to be participants in the salvation and to realize that the God of Israel is the one and only God. The final verse tells us that the witnesses and messengers from the nations are just as much part of God's chosen people as those whom they won over by their witness. Therefore they qualify for service in God's Holy Place.

Responsorial Psalm   **117 (116)**

℟ *Go out to the whole world;*
proclaim the Good News.
or *Alleluia!*

1 Alleluia!
O praise the Lord, all you nations,
acclaim him all you peoples! (R)

2 Strong is his love for us;
he is faithful for ever. (R)

This, the shortest of all the Psalms, is a formula of praise which shows clearly the universal aim of the Covenant. In calling all nations to worship the God of Israel, the Psalm picks up and echoes the sentiments of the first reading.

Second Reading   **Hebrews 12: 5–7, 11–13**

The author of Hebrews, writing to Christians who were faltering in their faith, probably because of persecution, prefaces his explanation of suffering as God's fatherly discipline with an exhortation to imitate Jesus. He quotes Proverbs 3: 11–12 which also speaks of suffering as part of one's training in God's discipline. This discipline, the author points out, is painful (as are the trials of his readers), but there is consolation in that these hardships will 'bear fruit in peace and goodness'. For this reason he exhorts his readers to endure, using the imagery of the racecourse, and then that of the road on which the people of God must journey.

Gospel   **Luke 13: 22–30**

The message of Jesus here is plain for all: the penalty for refusal is harsh. Whether few or many will be saved is a question that Jesus refuses to speculate upon; such matters are better left to the wisdom and mercy of God. One fact is urgent and clear: the Kingdom of God is already present, and is an open door. But that door is not so easily negotiable as to allow for idle speculation to replace determined action. It will not remain open indefinitely; the idle and the indifferent may well be too late. The people of Israel may have been the first to be given the promise, but if they do not act now their place will be taken by those who have accepted the gospel invitation. Indeed the standards of the Kingdom of heaven are not those of earth and so the complacent will meet many surprises.

Twenty-second Sunday in Ordinary Time

It is the humble who will find favour with God.

First Reading   **Ecclesiasticus 3: 17–20, 28–29**

The author of this book, writing about 190 BC speaks to us of the nature and advantages of humility. The epigrammatic style is typical of the Wisdom literature of the Old Testament (cf. Proverbs). 'My son' is a phrase often used by the teacher of wisdom when addressing a disciple, and does not imply parentage. The teacher points out that humility is especially important for those in a higher social stratum. Greatness must be accompanied by humility. One should be conscious of one's limitation and one's true position as a creature and sinner before God. The final verses draw a contrast between the truly wise man and the proud one, for whom there is no cure because evil has taken root in him.

Responsorial Psalm   **68 (67)**

℟ *In your goodness, O God, you prepared a home for the poor.*

1 The just shall rejoice at the presence of the God,
    they shall exult and dance for joy.
    O sing to the Lord, make music to his name;
    rejoice in the Lord, exult at his presence. (R)

2 Father of the orphan, defender of the widow,
    such is God in his holy place.
    God gives the lonely a home to live in;
    he leads the prisoners forth into freedom. (R)

3 You poured down, O God, a generous rain:
    when your people starved you gave them new life.
    It was there that your people found a home,
    prepared in your goodness, O God, for the poor. (R)

A response of praise to the God who shows himself as Saviour and Judge. We have pictures of different persons in need: the orphan, the widow, the lonely, the prisoner, and the starving. All of them get what they need from God.

Second Reading   Hebrews 12: 18–19, 22–24

The author now turns to the heavenly city, the goal of the Christian pilgrimage. He contrasts the two covenants, or orders of salvation, which are symbolized by two mountains: Mount Sinai, where the Old Covenant was made, and Mount Sion, the setting for the New Covenant. The scene of the old is on earth, and in describing it the author borrows phrases from Exodus 19 and 20 and Deuteronomy 4 and 5. The scene of the new is the heavenly Jerusalem, the place of Jesus' completed sacrifice upon which this New Covenant is founded. It is indeed this sacrifice of Jesus that has opened the heavenly sanctuary to the faithful. Already it is ours by anticipation, but in reality it awaits us in eternity: 'what you have come to is nothing known to the senses' but 'is Mount Sion, the city of the living God'.

Gospel   Luke 14: 1, 7–14

The material in this reading is found only in Luke's Gospel and has probably been placed in this context of the meal with the Pharisee by the evangelist himself. The key to the parable is found in the concluding sentence (v. 11). Jesus is not teaching social etiquette, but using an observation concerning good manners at table to teach about the Kingdom. Attendance at the heavenly banquet depends upon an invitation from God, who will invite only those who recognize their lowliness and their need for salvation. The scribes and Pharisees are thus quietly warned. Similarly, the second teaching of Jesus is not meant as practical advice. It tells rather that limited and interested love is worthless in the sight of God. Only those who act from motives of disinterested charity will reap their reward in the Kingdom.

Twenty-third Sunday in Ordinary Time

The inscrutability of God and the cost of discipleship are two of the subjects of today's readings.

First Reading   **Wisdom 9: 13–18**

The Hebrew poetic technique of using a couplet to express a single idea in different ways is well illustrated in this passage from Wisdom. The effect of the repetition is to throw more stress on the idea itself and so drive home the teaching more forcefully. In this reading a contrast is drawn between human intentions, which are hard enough to know, and the will of God which is so much greater and inscrutable. The emphasis, however, is both practical and ethical. Wisdom enables one to know the will of God in order to obey it. The author personifies Wisdom and identifies it with 'the Spirit of the Lord'. Though at this stage of revelation the author is not identifying these as distinct Persons in the Christian trinitarian sense, the teaching does supply the raw material for expressing the doctrine in due course.

Responsorial Psalm   **90 (89)**

℟ *O Lord, you have been our refuge*
  from one generation to the next.

1 You turn men back into dust
  and say: 'Go back, sons of men.'
  To your eyes a thousand years
  are like yesterday, come and gone,
  no more than a watch in the night. (R)

2 You sweep men away like a dream,
  like grass which springs up in the morning.
  In the morning it springs up and flowers:
  by evening it withers and fades. (R)

3 Make us know the shortness of our life
  that we may gain wisdom of heart.
  Lord, relent! Is your anger for ever?
  Show pity to your servants. (R)

4 In the morning, fill us with your love;
   we shall exult and rejoice all our days.
   Let the favour of the Lord be upon us:
   give success to the work of our hands. (R)

This community lament (cf. p. 12) contrasts the transitory nature of human life and eternity. This is not intended to lead to despair but rather to instil confidence in God, the Creator in whom we find refuge.

Second Reading   **Philemon 9–10, 12–17**

This short letter of Paul to Philemon should be read in its entirety, though the reading gives the central passages. Onesimus was a slave of Philemon and had become a Christian. At the time of writing, Paul was in prison and Onesimus, having run away from his master, was with him. This is the meaning of Paul's words that Philemon is 'deprived of him for a time'. In the letter Paul, who feels like the 'father' of Onesimus in that he brought him to faith, asks Philemon to welcome his slave back as a 'brother in the Lord'. His happiness should be greater because he is not only regaining the slave he had lost but also something more. 'A blood brother as well as a brother in the Lord' – a better translation of this would be: 'that is, speaking from both a human and a Christian point of view'.

Gospel   **Luke 14: 25–33**

This passage concerns the cost of discipleship. Luke has set two parables in the context of self-renunciation. He begins by an exhortation couched in the strongest terms. 'Hating' here is typical Semitic exaggeration and is simply a way of describing true detachment and total dedication. The twin parables drive home the lesson that discipleship requires commitment and cannot be undertaken simply on impulse, without careful consideration. The final verse was probably added by Luke himself, picking up the earlier reference to discipleship (v. 26) and is a practical consequence of the parables rather than their moral.

Twenty-fourth Sunday in Ordinary Time

Today's readings suggest that in the final analysis it is love and mercy that matter, before good order, religious rules or even justice.

First Reading   Exodus 32: 7–11, 13–14

While Moses is away speaking with God in the rarified heights of the mountain, the people, faced with uncertainty, press Aaron to fashion a golden calf to carry before them. When Aaron sees them hailing it as the 'god(s)' who had brought them up out of Egypt, he tries to direct the people's worship back to its true object. He builds an altar and proclaims a feast to the Lord. But when the people sacrifice and celebrate it is no longer clear who or what they are worshipping. God observes this rejection of his commandment and tells Moses that he will destroy them. Like Abraham at Sodom (Genesis 18–19), however, Moses intercedes with God. He reminds him of his promise to the patriarchs (e.g., Genesis 12: 2–3, 26: 2–5, 28: 13–15) and the Lord relents.

Two themes emerge in this story: (*a*) the ease with which the desire for certainty can lead to loss of true faith, and (*b*) the picture of God as one who is prepared to listen and respond, in mercy, to intercession.

Responsorial Psalm   51 (50)

℟ *I will leave this place and go to my father.*

1 Have mercy on me, God, in your kindness.
  In your compassion blot out my offence.
  O wash me more and more from my guilt
  and cleanse me from my sin. (R)

2 A pure heart create for me, O God,
  put a steadfast spirit within me.
  Do not cast me away from your presence,
  nor deprive me of your holy spirit. (R)

3 O Lord, open my lips
  and my mouth shall declare your praise.
  My sacrifice is a contrite spirit;
  a humbled, contrite heart you will not spurn. (R)

An individual lament (cf. p. 12), the fourth of the great 'Penitential Psalms'. The psalmist acknowledges his offence. His sacrifice is a contrite, humbled, heart. He looks confidently to God for mercy rather than rejection, for strengthening in a pure life rather than spiritual impoverishment.

Second Reading   **1 Timothy 1: 12–17**

Paul is writing to Timothy whom he has urged to stay in Ephesus in order to guide the Christian community there. The letter is much concerned with the practical ordering of the Christian life. Paul stresses, however, that what is important is not speculative discussions about the intricacies of traditional religious observance (the observance of the Mosaic Law) but the cultivation of 'love that issues from a pure heart and a good conscience and sincere faith'. Above all, the community must remember that religion is not a cosy set of rules for the 'just' but is a matter of life and death for sinners. Paul expresses his deep personal conviction of this truth. Before his conversion he had been foremost amongst the persecutors of Christ (i.e. through persecuting his followers), whereas he was now foremost amongst Christ's agents in the spread of the good news. At the centre of the gospel is God's mercy.

Gospel   **Luke 15: 1–32**

This reading expresses vividly in story form the point that we have seen Paul making to Timothy. It is a point made elsewhere in Luke's Gospel (e.g., 5: 27–32). The guardians of 'proper religion' condemn Jesus for receiving and eating with the 'sinners' and 'tax collectors' who come to him. Jesus replies by telling three parables, each of which conveys the message that at the heart of religion is God's love for those who have been 'lost' ('sinners') and his joy at their return to the community of faith. Each story ends with an invitation to rejoice, but it is the last that drives home the point by telling of the elder son's very understandable resentment at the favoured and seemingly 'unfair' treatment given to the returned 'prodigal'. Understandable that resentment may be, but for Jesus it is unacceptable. The scope of God's love and his joy at repentence cannot be limited by ordinary human ideas of what is fair or proper.

Twenty-fifth Sunday in Ordinary Time

Today's readings are concerned with wealth and privilege, poverty and social disadvantage.

First Reading   **Amos 8: 4-7**

Characteristic of the great prophet Amos is his fierce scorn for those who take advantage of the disadvantaged members of society. What triggers these angry words is not simply the fact that there are dishonest traders who 'rig' the weights and measures, who squeeze the poor to exact the utmost profit out of their weakness, buying them cheaply as slaves, and selling to them even the worthless part of the harvest. The real object of the anger is the fact that these same people who are so sharp in business are pillars of respectability who observe the religious feast days (the 'new moon' and the 'sabbath'). This is rank hypocrisy. They conveniently overlook the deeper moral demands of religious observance.

Responsorial Psalm   **113 (112)**

℟ *Praise the Lord, who raises the poor.*
 or *Alleluia!*

1 Alleluia!
  Praise, O servants of the Lord,
  praise the name of the Lord!
  May the name of the Lord be blessed
  both now and for evermore! (R)

2 High above all nations is the Lord,
  above the heavens his glory.
  Who is like the Lord, our God,
  who has risen on high to his throne
  yet stoops from the heights to look down,
  to look down upon heaven and earth? (R)

3 From the dust he lifts up the lowly,
  from the dungheap he raises the poor
  to set him in the company of princes,
  yes, with the princes of his people. (R)

A Psalm of praise lifts our thought to the greatness of God. Yet that very majesty only serves to emphasize the extent of his concern for the 'poor and lowly'. In God's eyes the poor and lowly are no less in rank than princes.

Second Reading   1 Timothy 2: 1–8

Paul gives priority to prayer for others. The community must not become preoccupied with its *own* problems. It must look outwards. Moreover, prayers should be made for all people, which includes kings and princes, those in high authority. (The letter is much concerned with the difficult question of how Christians should behave in a society which has marked divisions of class and privilege.) Christ's life and death was on behalf of *all* people. Note that Paul stresses his role as a teacher to the Gentiles, those outside his native Judaism. Christianity is no exclusive sect. He offers a glimpse of a harmonious, peaceful and *godly* society in which all will play a proper part, each respecting each.

Gospel   **Luke 16: 1–13**

This is a difficult parable, appearing to condone, indeed commend, dishonesty. The steward, faced with charges of embezzlement and the threat of dismissal, swiftly secures the friendship and goodwill essential to his future unemployment by putting his master's debtors in *his* debt – by marking down their outstanding bills. And yet, we are told, his master then commended him for the 'prudence' of his action. On top of which, Jesus appears to recommend the steward as a model of behaviour.

A traditional interpretation takes the moral details of the story to be unimportant. Only the main point matters – decisive, resourceful action in a desperate predicament is worthy of praise. Such 'prudent' application to the life of faith is demanded by Jesus.

Perhaps we should understand that Jesus (like Amos) is being sarcastic at the expense of the worldly characters of the story. When Jesus urges his listeners to follow the steward's example – buy your friends (to receive and look after you) through worldly-wise dishonesty – he does so with heavy irony, meaning exactly the opposite.

In the last few verses Jesus presses the point. A little faithfulness can go a long way, as can a little dishonesty. If you, like the steward, have not been honest and straightforward in your worldly involvement (the world of 'unrighteous mammon'), how can you expect to gain true (spiritual) wealth? The punchline is uncompromising: you cannot play fast and loose in pursuit of *worldly* wealth without destroying your *spiritual* wealth.

Twenty-sixth Sunday in Ordinary Time

Common to today's readings is a conviction that to be rich and to rule is to carry a heavy responsibility under God.

First Reading   **Amos 6: 1, 4–7**

The prophet's message of doom is directed to the *comfortable* members of society, the wealthy ruling class who live in Jerusalem (Zion), capital of the southern kingdom of Judah, and Samaria, capital of the northern kingdom of Israel. They are the ones to whom the ordinary people come – for justice and good government. Yet they live in luxury and idleness, totally out of touch with what is happening in the country. Amos has previously been speaking against the oppression and godlessness of the nation and predicting that conquest and exile lie ahead. Joseph, like David, was one of the great leaders of the past. By using the word 'Joseph' to describe the northern kingdom (made up of the tribes claiming descent from Joseph) Amos also implies that the leaders have betrayed a great tradition of leadership.

Responsorial Psalm   **146 (145)**

℟ *My soul, give praise to the Lord.*
  or *Alleluia!*

1 It is the Lord who keeps faith for ever,
   who is just to those who are oppressed.
   It is he who gives bread to the hungry,
   the Lord, who sets prisoners free. (R)

2 It is the Lord who gives sight to the blind,
   who raises up those who are bowed down.

It is the Lord who loves the just,
the Lord, who protects the stranger. (R)

3 He upholds the widow and orphan
but thwarts the path of the wicked.
The Lord will reign for ever,
Zion's God, from age to age. (R)

The Psalm echoes the concerns of Amos for the poor, the oppressed, and indeed for all who are at a special disadvantage in the community. It also picks up the theme of authority. If earthly rulers often fail in the exercise of their responsibility, God for his part is a king, *the* king, upon whom all may securely depend.

Second Reading   1 Timothy 6: 11–16

Paul has been talking of the snares and temptations associated with the desire to be rich, snares which have a habit of diverting people from the path of the faith. Only in holding fast and uncompromisingly to the qualities of a godly life will we lay hold of *real* life, life as it should and can be, 'eternal' life. Paul looked forward to the reappearance of Jesus, the End when Christ will give the final judgement. This belief adds an urgency to his exhortation to Timothy to avoid all compromise with 'worldliness'.

'Made the good confession' probably refers to Timothy's baptism where he would have made a public confession of faith, an assertion of the *truth*. Paul reminds Timothy of Jesus' courageous refusal to compromise before Pilate as a supreme example to follow. Nothing less than absolute commitment to the path of true faith is appropriate for anyone who would seek communion with 'the only Sovereign, the King of kings, and Lord of lords'.

Gospel   Luke 16: 19–31

(Note that the story is not intended to be taken as a literal depiction of the next world.) First we notice that the rich person is not openly charged with some special crime which merits his condemnation to Hades. Like the idle rich in Samaria, in Amos' prophecy, his fault emerges through the contrast of his sumptuous life-style with that of the less fortunate at his gate. The self-centredness of the rich man is wonderful to behold. In Hades he still wants to be waited upon, demanding that Lazarus soothe his parched tongue (reminding us, with a nice twist, of the dogs' service to Lazarus). The poor man is little more than a dog to the rich man. Clearly the rich man's crime lies as much in what he fails to do as in what he has done. He lacks concern for anyone but himself. Wealth carries responsibility. He fails utterly.

A second theme concerns Jesus' own preaching and teaching. The teaching of Moses and the prophets (such as Amos) is part of the rich man's own tradition. If he and his brothers cannot now recognize the force of its demands on their way of life, says Jesus, no amount of miracles will soften their hearts. The truth is there for them to see. The story is powerfully relevant to us who live after Christ's resurrection.

Twenty-seventh Sunday in Ordinary Time

In different ways today's readings urge us to serve God with an unwavering and patient faith.

First Reading   **Habakkuk 1: 2–3; 2: 2–4**

Habakkuk, acutely aware of terrible wrongdoing around him, has shouted 'violence', the cry for help of someone being assaulted. But no divine rescuer has appeared. He feels alone in a sea of injustice, and he cannot bear his sense of powerlessness in the face of it all. In the life of faith people will often despair that God has heard them, let alone answered their cry for help. The psalmist of Psalm 22 cries even more urgently than Habakkuk: 'My God, my God, why hast thou forsaken me?'

The answer lies in patient faith. 'I waited patiently for the Lord', says the psalmist of Psalm 40. So, in fact, with Habakkuk. God answers him with a vision (of coming destruction at the hands of the Babylonians) which is not quite what Habakkuk is expecting. Yet he takes up his stand in faith, looking to 'see what God will say to me' (2: 1). And God does respond, asking Habakkuk to record the vision so that all who read it may 'run' (in fear? or as a messenger to others?). Coming finally to the chief point – God does what he does in his own good time. The prophet must be patient and wait. The crucial thing is not to let go of his absolute commitment to right-doing. God's response to wickedness and injustice will come.

Responsorial Psalm 95 (94)

℟ *O that today you would listen to his voice!*
Harden not your hearts.

1 Come, ring out our joy to the Lord;
hail the rock who saves us.
Let us come before him, giving thanks,
with songs let us hail the Lord. (R)

2 Come in; let us bow and bend low;
let us kneel before the God who made us
for he is our God and we
the people who belong to his pasture,
the flock that is led by his hand. (R)

3 O that today you would listen to his voice!
'Harden not your hearts as at Meribah,
as on that day at Massah in the desert
when your fathers put me to the test;
when they tried me, though they saw my work.' (R)

God is utterly dependable. He is a rock. He is a shepherd. The mention of 'rock' reminds the psalmist of a story about Israel's wanderings in the wilderness after the exodus from Egypt. At Meribah the people, unable to find water, began to turn on Moses and to doubt not only God's goodwill but also his presence. In patient response, God provided water from a rock for all to drink.

Second Reading 2 Timothy 1: 6–8, 13–14

Paul, imprisoned in Rome and facing execution, encourages Timothy to maintain his 'sincere faith' (v. 5) and stand firm in his beliefs. He reminds Timothy that the office which he holds carries with it a gift from God which will enable him to carry out his tasks. We may recall God's empowering of Moses, called to confront

145

Pharaoh and lead Israel out of Egypt (Exodus 3–6). The task before Timothy is clearly a daunting one. But, says Paul, God is with him. A spirit of 'power and love and self-control' is given to him. The Holy Spirit dwells within him.

Gospel   Luke 17: 5–10

The disciples ask for their faith to be increased and in doing so reveal to Jesus an imperfect understanding. They think of faith as a matter of quantity. So Jesus offers insight through a typically colourful and humorous illustration. A seed-full of faith (so to speak) would provide power over a whole grown tree. With the smallest possible 'amount' of faith one can achieve the impossible. What more can one need? *Having* faith is what counts. At the same time, the absurdity of the particular illustration – getting a tree to transplant itself into the sea! – warns against taking the details literally. Jesus is *not* inviting Christians to become merely conjurors and magicians!

Furthermore, if in faith the disciples are empowered to do 'all that is commanded', they should not think that they are due some special reward. They will only have done their 'duty', like the servant in Jesus' next illustration. The disciples have been commanded to be faithful.

Twenty-eighth Sunday in Ordinary Time

Salvation is for all humankind.

First Reading   2 Kings 5: 14–17

Naaman was a Syrian general who enjoyed high favour with his king but suffered from leprosy. His wife's maid was an Israelite who had been carried off in a raid by the Syrians. She told her mistress of an Israelite prophet, a 'man of God' (Elisha), who she was sure could cure the leprosy of her new master. It is a classic story of the strange paths of faith. Eventually Naaman followed Elisha's odd-sounding instructions and was cured, but not without many hesitations, doubts, and surprises on the part of all concerned – except the man of God. Yet despite all his sidetracks on the way, Naaman did discover

God in the end, though still in his own imperfect way, unable to shake off the idea that a god was in some way territorial. So, with the aid of his mule-loads of Israelite soil, he worshipped the Lord!

Responsorial Psalm   **98 (97)**

℞ *The Lord has shown his salvation to the nations.*

1 Sing a new song to the Lord
for he has worked wonders.
His right hand and his holy arm
have brought salvation. (R)

2 The Lord has made known his salvation;
has shown his justice to the nations.
He has remembered his truth and love
for the house of Israel. (R)

3 All the ends of the earth have seen
the salvation of our God.
Shout to the Lord all the earth,
ring out your joy. (R)

This hymn of praise may remind us of the great prophecy of the exile (Isaiah 40–55). It celebrates a 'saving' act of God for Israel which has been witnessed by other nations.

Second Reading   **2 Timothy 2: 8–13**

From prison ('wearing fetters like a criminal') Paul challenges Timothy to take his share of suffering, if need be, in furtherance of the good news ('gospel') of Jesus Christ. Even if those who preach are enchained, the gospel itself (the 'word of God') can never be tied down.

The disciple of Jesus has a stark choice. He or she may endure everything for the sake of the gospel and gain new life with Jesus, or bow to the pressure of the world, deny him, and risk being denied by him. At stake is nothing less than life in eternal glory. But the challenge is not just directed to the individual, in this case Timothy, to consider his or her own interests. Paul sees his endurance in terms of others, the 'elect', all those called to Christ. Suffering for the sake of the gospel is above all suffering for the sake of others.

Gospel   **Luke 17: 11-19**

The area around the ancient capital of northern Israel, Samaria, had
been settled at the end of the eighth century BC by immigrants
brought in by the conquering Assyrians from far-away parts of the
Empire. For centuries afterwards the rest of the country, especially
the southern Judaeans, had regarded the people of Samaria with
suspicion and often hostility. They were not the 'true' people of God,
they said. Our present reading reminds us of the parable of the Good
Samaritan. There, unexpectedly, it was the 'foreigner' who stopped
to help. Here, unexpectedly, it is the 'foreigner' who alone comes
back to Jesus to thank him and, above all, to praise God. Like
Naaman, the Samaritan recognized the true source of the miracle –
God. For Jesus that was the sign of faith.

Twenty-ninth Sunday in Ordinary Time

God is with us. But do we fully draw upon his power?

First Reading   **Exodus 17: 8-13**

What exactly was Moses doing? Jewish and Christian commentators
have traditionally assumed that Moses was striking the attitude of
prayer. While he prayed the Israelites prospered; when he stopped
the tide turned against them. Another suggestion is that the hands
should be understood as the means of mediating power. Such a
conception was common in the ancient Near East and is reflected
elsewhere in the Bible. On this view Moses mediates the intervention
of God in the battle. The raising of his hands symbolizes the power of
God unleashed on the enemy. In either case the point is that in the
final analysis it is not the Israelites who win the battle but God.
Nonetheless the story also makes clear that for there to be success the
Israelites (and Moses in particular) had to play their part.

That God should seek to destroy the Amalekites should be understood in the context of Israel's struggle for survival in the wilderness.
The Amalekites (whom the Church Fathers often took to be symbo-
lic of evil) had threatened Israel's existence, and in a sense that threat

was a threat to God himself. Sometimes there is no room for half-measures – as Jesus himself often observed.

Responsorial Psalm 121 (120)

℟ *Our help is in the name of the Lord,*
who made heaven and earth.

1 I lift up my eyes to the mountains:
from where shall come my help?
My help shall come from the Lord
who made heaven and earth. (R)

2 May he never allow you to stumble!
Let him sleep not, your guard.
No, he sleeps not nor slumbers,
Israel's guard. (R)

3 The Lord is your guard and your shade;
at your right side he stands.
By day the sun shall not smite you
nor the moon in the night. (R)

4 The Lord will guard you from evil,
he will guard your soul.
The Lord will guard your going and coming
both now and for ever. (R)

God's presence with us is like a soldier to rescue us, a tree to shade us. He will guard us from the ravages of evil.

Second Reading 2 Timothy 3: 14–4: 2

The 'sacred writings' ('holy scripture') of which Paul speaks were probably the books of the Old Testament, though it is possible that some new Christian literature was also intended. In exhorting Timothy to stand firm by his beliefs, Paul has repeatedly reminded him that he does not stand alone. For example, Paul's own experience should be an encouragement to him. Here he points to another source of strength. Whatever the situation in which he finds himself in the course of his work, he will always be able to draw insight and encouragement from the Scriptures. God is with him in the Scriptures, for the scriptures are 'inspired' by God.

Gospel   **Luke 18: 1–8**

This parable belongs to a group of sayings on the coming of the Kingdom of God. The characters of the parable are a widow, who represents the poor and needy in society, and a judge, who is said to fear neither God nor man – he is a hard and 'worldly' man in a position of power. The widow asks him to secure her rights against an opponent who we may guess has taken advantage of her weak position. The judge is not interested in someone of such lowly status but is gradually worn down by her persistence until he does what she has asked and 'vindicates' her. If the unrighteous judge will respond thus to the widow's persistence, how much more will (righteous) God answer the constant prayer of his own people (his 'elect') and vindicate them?

The contrast makes a further point. May we not feel confident that, unlike the judge, God will act with all appropriate speed? (The point was especially pertinent to those in the early Church who were suffering persecution and looking for an imminent *parousia* or second coming, the End which would see the fulfilment of the Kingdom.)

Thirtieth Sunday in Ordinary Time

Today's readings point to the need for honest self-assessment by the professing Christian.

First Reading   **Ecclesiasticus 35: 12–14, 16–19**

The writer has condemned worship by those whose everyday life is in fact ungodly and oppressive. For him, keeping the (moral) law clearly takes precedence over ritualistic ceremony. ('Keeping the law is worth many offerings; to heed the commandments is to sacrifice a thank-offering', 35: 1.) Nevertheless, sincere worship *is* a significant part of the religious life. In our passage he continues the theme, noting not only the uselessness of insincere ('unrighteous') worship but also its attendant risk, for the God who receives worship is also a scrupulous judge who 'executes judgement' – in favour of the righteous and against the unrighteous. To try to 'bribe' God by offering worship built upon an unrighteous and uncaring life is to compound the crime. God sees through all such people and will treat them as they have treated others. Those who humbly and sincerely persist in prayer will be visited with the comfort of God's presence.

Responsorial Psalm   34 (33)

℟ *This poor man called; the Lord heard him.*

1 I will bless the Lord at all times,
    his praise always on my lips;
    in the Lord my soul shall make its boast.
    The humble shall hear and be glad. (R)

2 The Lord turns his face against the wicked,
    to destroy their remembrance from the earth.
    The just call and the Lord hears
    and rescues them in all their distress. (R)

3 The Lord is close to the broken-hearted;
    those whose spirit is crushed he will save.
    The Lord ransoms the souls of his servants.
    Those who hide in him shall not be condemned. (R)

A thanksgiving for the answering of prayers. Like Ecclesiasticus, it proclaims belief in the ultimate dependability of God as the one whose place is with the distressed and broken-hearted.

Second Reading   2 Timothy 4: 6–8, 16–18

Paul sees the end approaching fast. He is on the point of being 'poured out as a libation (drink-offering)'. That is to say, his final sacrifice to God, his supreme act of worship, will be the offering of his life to God as a witness to his truth. And he is utterly confident that the Lord, the righteous judge, will confirm his (Paul's) righteousness, as also that of all who have enjoyed the faith ('loved his appearing'). His confidence in the Lord draws strength from the fact that in the early days of his trial God alone stood by him, enabling him to continue his witness. But though he was at that time 'rescued from the lion's mouth' he does not expect to be saved from death now. Rather he will be rescued from what really matters, from 'every evil', so that in *righteousness*, untainted by evil, he may be with the Lord in his 'heavenly' kingdom.

Gospel   **Luke 18: 9–14**

Jesus warns against shallow self-satisfaction. The Pharisee claims righteousness on the basis, first, of what he has not done (resorted to extortion or injustice, committed adultery, been in a job that was not 'respectable') and, second, of what he has done by way of religious 'observance' – he has fasted regularly and given 'tithes' (put money in the collection plate!). For him that is righteousness. We may wonder whether the author of Ecclesiasticus would have been impressed. The tax collector, on the other hand, simply confesses his lowliness. He humbly asks for mercy. He has no illusions about himself.

Jesus' final comment stresses that it is humility that counts above all. Out of humility can yet grow Paul's conviction of righteousness. Out of humility comes the tax collector's recognition of unrighteousness, a recognition which makes him acceptable to God.

Thirty-first Sunday in Ordinary Time

Who will receive the Kingdom?

First Reading   **Wisdom 11: 22–12: 2**

All power belongs to God – 'For it is always in thy power to show great strength, and who can withstand the might of thy arm?' 11: 21 – because the whole world is as nothing before him. Nevertheless, a totality of power, the possibility of doing all things, offers God the freedom to be merciful. The passage stresses that God as creator loves his creation and is therefore not only able but willing to spare humankind. The world exists because of his love. God's mercy allows 'those who trespass' the chance to repent, to see the folly of wickedness and to be freed.

Responsorial Psalm   **145 (144)**

℟ *I will bless your name for ever,*
   O God my King.

1 I will give you glory, O God my King,
   I will bless your name for ever.
   I will bless you day after day
   and praise your name for ever. (R)

2 The Lord is kind and full of compassion,
   slow to anger, abounding in love.
   How good is the Lord to all,
   compassionate to all his creatures. (R)

3 All your creatures shall thank you, O Lord,
   and your friends shall repeat their blessing.
   They shall speak of the glory of your reign
   and declare your might, O God. (R)

4 The Lord is faithful in all his words
   and loving in all his deeds.
   The Lord supports all who fall
   and raises all who are bowed down. (R)

This hymn of praise (cf. p. 12) also celebrates God's power and compassion. These support those who fall; and the psalmist has in mind here not only the fall of material misfortune but also of sin.

Second Reading   **2 Thessalonians 1: 11–2: 2**

Paul's letter is addressed to a Christian community which was suffering persecution. He has assured them that their suffering does not go unheeded by God. Prominent in the church's mind was the idea that the end of the present age was at hand, with a return of Christ in glory expected at any time. This sense of approaching judgement perhaps gave believers a heightened consciousness of the radical choice that confronted them in the way they lived their lives. On the other hand, it could also distract them from the more mundane demands of a faithful life into an excited preoccupation with discerning signs and wonders. Paul urges caution. What counts is that they, in God's power, 'fulfil every good resolve and work of faith'.

Gospel   **Luke 19: 1–10**

The rich tax collector was despised by 'righteous' members of the community who considered what he did for his living to be unethical and disloyal. He shows a remarkable interest in Jesus, to the extent of climbing a tree in order to see him. But the real initiative comes from Jesus, who uncannily marks him out and invites himself to Zacchaeus' house.

The tax collector's joy is characteristic of all who receive Jesus and recognize the Kingdom of God. By contrast the onlookers can only murmur their self-righteous indignation. We may remember the contrast between the Pharisee and the tax collector last Sunday. Here also, it is the 'sinner' who genuinely sees into his own condition. Face to face with Jesus he recognizes him as 'Lord' (or 'Master') and, implicitly confessing his wrongdoing, vows not only to make restitution to those he has wronged but also to give not a 'tithe' (tenth) of his wealth but *half* to the poor.

In verse 9 Jesus makes the point that to gain salvation as one of God's chosen people is not just a matter of natural descent or professed religious adherence. Zacchaeus was no doubt a Jew by descent. What makes him a true son of Abraham is his active reception of the message of the Kingdom. Members of a 'chosen' community who assume salvation assume too much. The lesson is one for Christians as well as Jews.

Thirty-second Sunday in Ordinary Time

The readings set the demands of faithful service beside the promise of glory.

First Reading   **2 Maccabees 7: 1–2, 9–14**

About 168 BC a new line of 'Hellenistic' (Greek) rulers sought to impress on the Jews pagan practices, forcing subjection by deliberately making those who resisted break their own religious laws. Thus in our reading the king seeks submission by trying to enforce the eating of pig meat, which of course was repugnant to the pious Jew.

The story recounts the martyrdom of a mother and her seven sons, who steadfastly refuse to comply with the king's command. As the account moves in turn from martyr to martyr, each making a speech of defiance, there emerges a striking affirmation of God's power to raise to life again. They are prepared to die rather than back-track on their faith. They go to their deaths in the hope of an everlasting renewal of life.

Responsorial Psalm   17 (16)

℟ *I shall be filled, when I awake,*
   with the sight of your glory, O Lord.

1 Lord, hear a cause that is just,
   pay heed to my cry.
   Turn your ear to my prayer:
   no deceit is on my lips. (R)

2 I kept my feet firmly in your paths;
   there was no faltering in my steps.
   I am here and I call, you will hear me, O God.
   Turn your ear to me; hear my words. (R)

3 Hide me in the shadow of your wings.
   As for me, in my justice I shall see your face
   and be filled, when I awake, with the sight of your glory. (R)

The dominant note of this 'lament' (cf. p. 12) is the psalmist's certainty that he will be heard. The shadow of his peril will give way to the shadow of God's 'wings' and from the night of trouble he will awake to God's glory.

Second Reading   2 Thessalonians 2: 16–3: 5

Paul has warned the people of the Thessalonian church against being deluded into accepting false authority, however powerful and impressive it might appear. Typically he tells them simply to 'stand firm and hold to the traditions' which he had taught them (v. 15). In our reading he calls forth a blessing upon them, for he knows that God will give the comfort and hope needed for their work. Similarly he asks that they pray for him and his colleagues. For he, too, faces difficulties. In the end, however, what matters is that 'the Lord is faithful; he will strengthen you and guard you from evil'.

Gospel   **Luke 20: 27–38**

A belief in the resurrection life was a doctrine Jesus shared with the Pharisees (Luke 14: 14). This view, however, was contested by the Sadducees, another major group in Jewish religion. In our passage they attempt to ridicule the belief by posing a 'test-case'. In the (rather far-fetched!) instance of the seven brothers, obliged by traditional 'levirate' law to marry the same woman in turn as each died, a resurrection would imply a final situation of one woman with a number of husbands. The force of the argument is that a belief which leads to such a suggestion must be false.

Jesus replies in two ways. He attacks the idea that the resurrection life ('that age') is simply an extension of this present life ('this age'). Secondly, he offers a counter-argument from Scripture. The fact that the book of Exodus ('Moses') has God describe himself to Moses as the God of Abraham, Isaac and Jacob, only makes sense (he argues) if these patriarchs, apparently long since dead, were in some sense alive.

Thirty-third Sunday in Ordinary Time

The readings are concerned with the 'day of the Lord'.

First Reading   **Malachi 3: 19–20**

For centuries before Christ, prophets in Israel spoke of a great day which was coming, a 'day of the Lord', when God would intervene in the world, making a radical break between the existing age and a new age to come. Humankind would stand under judgement. It would be a time when the good would be separated from the evil. The prophet Malachi takes up this theme, at first picturing the day in terms of flames. Fire may be destructive or beneficial. The evildoers will find the day burning like an oven and themselves the stubble which fuels the fire! The righteous will find the day lit and warmed by a great sun which will radiate new life. They shall be filled with joy like calves set free from their night stalls, leaping into the open fields at dawn.

Responsorial Psalm   98 (97)

℟ *The Lord comes to rule the peoples with fairness.*

1 Sing psalms to the Lord with the harp
  with the sound of music.
  With trumpets and the sound of the horn
  acclaim the King, the Lord. (R)

2 Let the sea and all within it thunder;
  the world, and all its peoples.
  Let the rivers clap their hands
  and the hills ring out their joy
  at the presence of the Lord. (R)

3 For the Lord comes,
  comes to rule the earth.
  He will rule the world with justice
  and the peoples with fairness. (R)

An enthronement hymn (cf. p. 13), perhaps originally used in connection with the enthronement of a new (earthly) king, but now celebrating the rule of the King of kings, the Lord God.

Second Reading   2 Thessalonians 3: 7–12

We have noted in an earlier reading (31st Sunday) Paul's concern lest a preoccupation with the second coming should undermine the Thessalonians' commitment to the ongoing work of the church. The present passage (and v. 6) suggests that some of the community had indeed succumbed to idleness, no doubt believing that since the End was at hand all further work was irrelevant. Paul condemns such a view and offers his own practice (cf. Acts 18: 3 – he was a tentmaker) as an example to be followed still.

Gospel   Luke 21: 5–19

Jesus has earlier spoken of the coming desolation of the Temple (19: 43f.) – which in fact took place in AD 70. Here he warns his listeners not to take the destruction of the Temple as a sign that the End would follow immediately. There will be many who will announce, falsely, the nearness of the End, appealing to this or that sign or portent. The signs frequently associated with the End-time ('wars and tumults') are indeed signs, but not such that the observer can know that the End will be at once. Thus the discourse makes clear that a measure of mystery or ambiguity must be reckoned with in speaking of this time. More certain, however, is the bitter fact that the faithful will be persecuted for their beliefs. Yet paradoxically, though 'some of you they will put to death', 'not a hair of your head will perish'. There will be new life for all who patiently endure in the name of Christ.

Christ the King (Last Sunday of the year)

First Reading   2 Samuel 5: 1–3

Following Saul's death, the people of Judah in the south made David king over their part of the country. A war followed between the supporters of David and those who wished the house of Saul to continue in power. Our reading tells of the outcome, when representatives of all the tribes of Israel came to David at Hebron, made a covenant (treaty or contract) with him, and anointed him king. David's reign signified a kind of ideal age for later Israelites. Within a generation the country had split into rival kingdoms. Nor again do we see king and people entering freely into a covenant bond. David was early designated by God, through his prophet Samuel, as shepherd and leader of Israel. In later times there emerged the belief that a new and remarkable 'anointed one' (Messiah or Christ) would arise who would be of the Davidic line, a 'son of David'.

Responsorial Psalm   122 (121)

℟ *I rejoiced when I heard them say:*
  'Let us go to God's house.'

1 I rejoiced when I heard them say:
  'Let us go to God's house.'

And now our feet are standing
within your gates, O Jerusalem. (R)

2 Jerusalem is built as a city
strongly compact.
It is there that the tribes go up,
the tribes of the Lord. (R)

3 For Israel's law it is,
there to praise the Lord's name.
There were set the thrones of judgement
of the house of David. (R)

A pilgrimage Psalm (cf. p. 13) sung by those making pilgrimages to Jerusalem, which became a central place of worship from the time when David established the city as his capital.

Second Reading   **Colossians 1: 11–20**

Paul prays that the 'faithful brethren at Colossae' may gain strength from Christ and that they give thanks to God for effecting their transformation from the creatures of sin and darkness to the subjects of Christ's kingdom of loving forgiveness and light.

But to speak of Christ's might and kingdom is to speak of God's power and creation. Paul moves easily into one of the great hymns of the New Testament (vv. 15–20). Christ is pre-eminent in the whole universe. The hymn draws upon the Old Testament understanding of the wisdom of God (treated poetically almost as a person; cf. Proverbs 8). Using traditional terminology, the hymn conveys a vision of Christ as the embodiment of God's wisdom in the continuing creative work of God, and in reconciliation.

Gospel   **Luke 23: 35–43**

Placed on the cross with a criminal on either side of him, Jesus utters his astonishing prayer, 'Father, forgive them' (v. 34). Now Luke looks more closely at the various people present. The ordinary people watch, apparently in non-commital silence. The religious rulers, however, as well as the soldiers and one of the criminals, mock the idea that he could be the expected Messiah ('anointed king', the 'Christ'). If he is God's specially chosen one (say the religious officials) or a *real* king (say the soldiers) then he surely has it in his power to prevent his execution. One criminal, perhaps having momentarily hoped that Jesus would perform some miracle that would rescue them from their terrible predicament, vents his fear in sarcasm. By contrast, the other criminal has clearly looked beyond himself. He has considered the stark injustice of Jesus' condemnation. No doubt, too, he has listened in awe to Jesus' prayer, 'Father, forgive them'. And because he had opened his heart and mind to Jesus he knows this strange man beside him to be someone truly remarkable.

So the second criminal recognizes Jesus as the kingly Messiah, not by witnessing some great miracle or by being materially helped in any way, but simply by looking upon Jesus' suffering and hearing his message of forgiveness. Jesus responds immediately to his faith by offering him the spiritual reassurance that he desperately needs to sustain him through a tortured death: 'Today you will be with me in Paradise'.

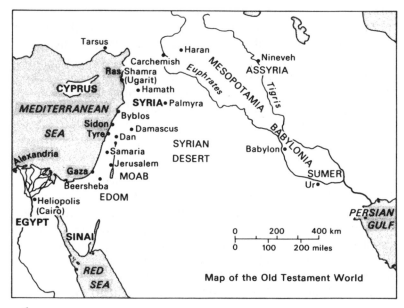

Map of the Old Testament World

Chronological Table I

A Chart of Old Testament History and Literature

The purpose of the chart is to help the reader by co-ordinating the history and the literature. It is not possible to be precise about the dates of the literature, nor does a suggested date rule out the possibility of additions to completed books (as evidenced by the additions to Daniel and Esther in the Greek versions).

History	Literature
1 The Patriarchal Age (2000*–1300* BC)	
2 The Age of Moses, Joshua and Judges (1300*–1000* BC)	Judges ch. 5 1100* BC
3 Samuel, Saul, David and Solomon (1050–931)	Oldest of the Psalms and other poetry 1200–950*
4 Pre-exilic Period (931–587)	Oldest prose parts of the Pentateuch (950–850)
a. The Divided Monarchy	Amos 760–750*
b. The Assyrian destruction of the Northern Kingdom 722/721	Hosea 745–725*
	Isaiah 740–701*
	Early prose parts of Joshua–Judges–Samuel–Kings 800–700*
	Micah 725–690*
c. Reign of Josiah 640–609	Zephaniah 630–625*
	Habakkuk 625–600*
	First edition of Deuteronomy and deuteronomic writings
d. The Fall of Assyrian Nineveh to the Babylonians 612 BC	Nahum 612–610*
	Jeremiah 626–586
e. The Babylonian Invasion of Judah 598	
f. Destruction of Judah and the Exile to Babylonia 587	

* *approximate dates*

5 The Exilic Period (587–539)	Passages in Jeremiah
	Ezekiel 593*–560*
a. The Persian conquest of	Second Isaiah (40–55) 550*–520*
Babylonia 539	
b. The Return from Exile 539*–516	Further compilations of elements in
	Pentateuch
6 The Post-Exilic Period (530*–	Haggai 520
167)	Zechariah 520–518
a. Persian Period 538–333	Malachi, Joel (?), Obadiah 500–450*
b. Careers of Ezra and Nehemiah	Third Isaiah (?) 500–450
450*	Priestly completion of the Penta-
	teuch 450–400
	Compilation of Proverbs 400*
	Job 450–350* (or possibly earlier)
	Jonah, Ruth 425*
	Ezra–Nehemiah–Chronicles 375–250*
	Possible final editing of prophetic
	books
c. Greek Period 333–167	Ecclesiastes 275–250*
	Translation of the Pentateuch into
	Greek 250*
	Daniel 165*

Chronological Table II

A Chart of New Testament History and Literature

It is generally accepted that all the New Testament works were written before *c.* 125, though it is difficult to be specific and dates given, therefore, are approximate.

Church History and Literature		Jewish History	
Birth of Jesus	6–4 BC (?)	Herod the Great	37–4 BC
		Herod Antipas (Tetrarch of Galilee)	4 BC–AD 39
		Archelaus (Ethnarch in Judea)	4 BC–AD 6
		Philip (Ethnarch of Ituraea)	4 BC–AD 34
		Caiaphas (High Priest)	AD 18–36
		Pontius Pilate (Roman Procurator in Judea)	26–36
Preaching of John the Baptist	27 (?)		
Ministry of Jesus	28–29 (?)		
Conversion of Paul	33–35 (?)		
		Herod Agrippa (King of Judea; from 41 king of the whole country)	37–44
James, son of Zebedee, executed; Peter imprisoned	41 (?)		
Paul in S. Galatia	47–49 (?)		
Paul in Corinth	50–51		
1 Thessalonians	51		
2 Thessalonians	51		
Paul in Ephesus	52–54	M. Antonius Felix (Procurator in Judea)	52–60
		M. Julius Agrippa II (Part of Galilee and	
Galatians	54–57	Peraea)	53
Paul arrested in Jerusalem	56		

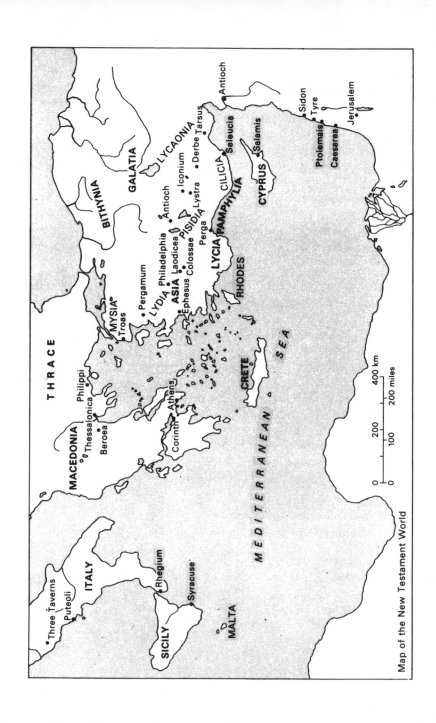

Map of the New Testament World

1 Corinthians	57		
2 Corinthians	57		
Romans	58		
Philippians late 50's early 60's			
		Porcius Festus (Procurator in Judea)	60–61
Paul in Rome	60		
Philemon	61–63		
Ephesians★	61–63		
Colossians★	61–63		
James	62 (?)		
Death of James	62		
1 Peter	64 (?)		
Martyrdom of Peter and Paul	64 (?)		
MARK	65		
1 Timothy★	65		
Titus★	65		
2 Timothy★	66–67		
Christians flee to Pella	66–67		
Hebrews	60's (?)	Jewish war with Rome	66–70
		Fall of Jerusalem	70
MATTHEW	70's, 80's (?)		
LUKE	70's, 80's (?)	Masada falls; end of Jewish revolt	73
Acts	70's, 80's (?)		
Jude	70's, 90's (?)		
James	80's (?)		
Hebrews	80's (?)		
JOHN	90's		
1 John	90's		
2 John	90's		
3 John	90's		
Apocalypse (Revelation)	90's		
2 Peter	100–125	Synod of Jamnia (fixed Old Testament Canon)	*c.* 100

★Authorship of these epistles questioned. If not Pauline then a later date, approx. 80's, is assigned.

Some Aids to Further Study

There are several series of commentaries that will be found helpful. They give introductory articles dealing with general background and also section by section comment.

The Torch Commentary (SCM Press). Usually these commentaries are short, in pocket-size paperbacks. Convenient and worth consulting.

The Cambridge Bible Commentary. This is a commentary on the New English Bible, the text of which is included. Fairly brief and generally very clear. The hardback edition is now expensive, but the series is also published in paper-back.

The New Century Bible (Oliphants). A fuller commentary than the preceding two both as regards introduction and explanation of the text. The text is RSV but not included.

One-volume commentaries which may be found useful include:

Peake's Commentary on the Bible. Ed. Matthew Black (Nelson 1963) Still reasonably priced.

The Interpreter's One Volume Commentary on the Bible (Collins and Abingdon).

The Jerome Biblical Commentary (Chapman and Prentice Hall). Good material but sometimes difficult to track down. Unfortunately now very expensive. R.C.

The New Catholic Commentary on Holy Scripture (Nelson). Generally well laid out and easy to follow. Still reasonably priced.

These one-volume commentaries contain useful introductory articles of general biblical background and relevance as well as commentary on the individual books. Some useful general introductions include:

Stuart Blanch, *For All Mankind* (Murray/BRF and Oxford, N.Y.). Short but lively and clear.

William Barclay, *Introducing the Bible* (BRF/IBRA). Much information in an easy style.

A. E. Harvey, *Something Overheard: an Introduction to the New Testament* (BRF). Again a short but clear introduction.

Claus Westermann, *Handbook to the Old Testament* (SPCK large paperbacks). This is precisely what it says, a handbook, and a very useful one.

The most useful Bible atlases are:

Oxford Bible Atlas, ed. Herbert May (OUP). Very clear maps and a good deal of information in the accompanying articles.

H. H. Rowley, *Student's Bible Atlas*. Good clear maps. Very reasonably priced.

L. H. A. Grollenberg, *Shorter Atlas of the Bible* (Nelson, now also Penguin). Not all that many maps but a fair amount of interesting material in the text.

This is only a brief selection of books for further study. Larger and more detailed bibliographies are to be found in many of the titles listed here.